Early praise for *Shanda*

"The search for his *Yiddishe* heart takes Neal Karlen from self-loathing to self-examination to self-respect. On the way he enlightens us about Jewish outlaws, the finer points of shticking, and the truth about Hasids. Meshugenner? A little, but this guy is 100 percent mensch."

> —Peggy Orenstein, author of *Flux: Women on Sex, Work, Love, Kids & Life in a Half-Changed World*

"Karlen's affecting and funny book turns the notion of 'It's hard to be a Jew' on its head. What's hard to be is half a Jew. I wanted this exceptional pair—rabbi and student—to keep studying, joking, praying, and talking to each other. Many an American man and woman will recognize themselves."

> —Ruchama King, author of *Seven Blessings*

"An irreverent account of Karlen's return to his deepest self. You will get *nachas* from reading about his transformation."

> —Sherri Mandel, author of *The Blessing of a Broken Heart* and cofounder of the Koby Mandel Foundation

"This is a zesty memoir of spiritual adventure. Volubly ambivalent, our hero protests all the way through his struggle to forge an authentic Jewish identity. It is both entertaining and moving to watch this self-proclaimed 'shtick-meister' grow into a sweetly serious man. . . . A wild ride of a book: comic, anguished, smart-alecky, exuberant, and poignant by turn."

> —Brigitte Frase, winner of the National Book Critics Circle's Nona Balakian Excellence in Reviewing Award

ALSO BY NEAL KARLEN

Slouching Towards Fargo: A Two-Year Saga of Sinners and
St. Paul Saints at the Bottom of the Bush Leagues with
Bill Murray, Darryl Strawberry, Dakota Sadie, and Me

Babes in Toyland: The Making and Selling of a Rock and Roll Band

Take My Life, Please! (with Henny Youngman)

SHANDA

The Making
and Breaking of
a Self-Loathing Jew

NEAL KARLEN

A TOUCHSTONE BOOK
Published by Simon & Schuster
New York   London   Toronto   Sydney

TOUCHSTONE
Rockefeller Center
1230 Avenue of the Americas
New York, NY 10020

TOUCHSTONE and colophon are registered trademarks
of Simon & Schuster, Inc.

For information regarding special discounts for bulk purchases,
please contact Simon & Schuster Special Sales at 1-800-456-6798
or business@simonandschuster.com

Designed by Helene Berinsky

Manufactured in the United States of America

1   3   5   7   9   10   8   6   4   2

Library of Congress Cataloging-in-Publication Data
Karlen, Neal.
Shanda: the making and breaking of a self-loathing Jew/Neal Karlen.
p.   cm.
"A Touchstone book."
1. Karlen, Neal—Religion. 2. Jews—Minnesota—Biography.
3. Journalists—Minnesota—Biography. 4. Jewish journalists—Minnesota—
Biography. 5. Friedman, Manis. 6. Habad. 7. Self-hate (Psychology.
8. Self-acceptance—Religious aspects—Judaism. 9. Jews—Return to
Orthodox Judaism. I. Title.
F610.3.K37A3   2004
296'.092—dc22 [B]   2004048141

ISBN 0-7432-1382-3

For my own rebbe, Suzanne Gluck,
who's always led me out of the desert

ACKNOWLEDGMENTS

First and foremost I want to thank Doris Cooper, senior editor. For almost three years, Doris has labored heroically, as either Maimonides or Casey Kasem had it, to keep my feet on the ground while still reaching for the stars. Her diligent line and big-picture edits of the manuscript, through all its drafts, kept me both from drifting off to the Pluto of my tangents and focused on what exactly I wanted to say. She believed in the book before I even knew what it was, fought for it when other editors would have thrown up their hands, and kept me going whenever I just wanted to surrender. A *groiser dank,* Doris, to put it mildly, and if you don't mind my using Yiddish and Latin in the same sentence, *you* are truly the one who's *sui generis.*

Second, third, and fourth, I want to thank Suzanne Gluck's assistants, Caroline Sparrow at ICM and Emily Nurkin; Christine Price; and alas, at last, Erin Malone at William Morris, for their kindness to someone they'd never met. All four were patient while I could hear ninety-seven phones going off in the background and opened the gate whenever I needed an audience with *tutti di capo tutti* to discuss anything from dough to girlfriends. Christine deserves special praise for help in bringing the book to a close and for understanding the kabbalistic meaning of stones.

At Simon & Schuster, I would also like to thank publishers David Rosenthal and Mark Gompertz and Doris's assistant, Sara Schapiro, who helped in bringing this baby home and made me laugh when I was filling out applications for correspondence schools on the back of matchbook covers. Simon & Schuster lawyer Elisa Rivlin was both precise, funny, and strict, and Cynthia Merman, the copy editor, found idiotic gaffes.

I would also like to thank Rabbi Manis Friedman and his wife, Chana, who welcomed me into their home with no idea what I was doing or wanted, and never asked. I'd sometimes disappear for months without a word, yet Rabbi Friedman's smile never broke. Also sharing their kindness and stories around the Friedman home were Moitel, Chaya, Nissan, Muschka, and too many others to name. I hope you all sense in this book the respect and admiration I feel for each of you.

Lu Lippold, Bruce Johnson, and Elianna Lippold-Johnson did me the critical favor of lending me their daughter and sister Mira and their dining room table, so I could see if I still had the chops to tutor a child for her bat mitzvah. They didn't worry what I was up to even when I showed Mira the Jewish aspects of the film *The Big Lebowski* or spent a lesson talking about Sandy Koufax as part of her training. I thank them, too, for always feeding me the best home-cooked meal I'd had all week.

Peggy Orenstein, who, in her previous life before becoming a big-shot writer, was a big-shot Torah reader, did me the huge favor of responding to my call of "I need help with a haftarah reading I have to teach to Mira next week!" As gawkers looked on in the French Meadow Bakery, Peggy then tutored me not only in all the notes but also in the portion I had to teach. *Du bis a mentsch.*

My parents, Dr. Markle and Charlotte Karlen, and my siblings, Bonnie and Bruce, like the Friedmans never had any idea what I was doing all these years yet never wavered in their support. I hope all of you take from this book the respect, admiration, and love I meant.

The Southern Baptist minister James Nelson tutored me in Kierkegaard, while the Reverend Richard Mammen explained the Christian reading of Cain and Abel. And thank you, Jodes Nelson and Tricia Mammen, for letting me take your husbands away.

Rabbi Richard Rabowitz gave me further insight into Judaic theology, and Amanda Siegel tutored me in Shylock's big speech, in Yiddish, while Pam Kennedy did the same in English. Rabbi Tim Appelo and his wife, Tori, explicated the meaning of a *Yiddishe hartz*. Hannah Kampf and Marcey and Norman Bolter taught me the reality of the concentration camps. Abbie Kane fed me chicken soup when the Friedmans or Lippold-Johnsons weren't around.

Chuck and Soraya Strouse let me stay at their house in Miami every time winter hit Minnesota and never asked, "Aren't you done yet?" The rebbetzin Dara Moskowitz not only kept me sane but always thought I was writing another book.

Professor Art Simon and his wife, psychotherapist Barbara Berger, gave me much needed insight into the psychology of Judaica, and Hillery Borton saved this book by telling me something two and a half years into it.

Mordecai Spector, editor of *The American Jewish World,* provided me with the critical contemporary proof that Rabbi Moshe Feller indeed laid tefillin with Sandy Koufax on that extra-fateful Yom Kippur in 1965 when Koufax stayed in his room at the St. Paul Hotel instead of pitching.

My accountant and great friend Brian Tunkel saved me when the sharks were circling.

Bill Bates, Chris Kleman, and Bill Tyler helped me fix my computer the many times it blew up. Emily Goldberg, whose spiritual and emotional contributions to this book are inestimable, let me use her computer for weeks while she was in the middle of finishing her film. Tom Bartel and his wife, Kris, finally took *rachmones* on me and lent me their spare computer and introduced me to Sarah. Nick and Laura let me "see the baby" whenever I needed. And Andrea Michaels was on her mark.

Lori Gottlieb read the entire book in a week and revealed to me a spirit I'd never seen before. Emily Gordon read the manuscript and helped in a myriad ways during the publishing endgame. Shannon Olson read an early draft of this book and showed me that shtick isn't necessarily funny. Heather McElhatton graciously allowed me to substitute her name for my ex-wife's.

My writing students at the University of Minnesota School of Journalism taught me as much as the rabbis with their quizzical inquiries into the meaning of it all. Professor Nancy Roberts let me have at them.

Mrs. Shirley Dworsky and the St. Paul Hadassah let me discuss the book in progress and gave me their uncensored opinions. Jeffrey Schachtman at the Minneapolis Jewish Community Center let me do the same and kept the audience from throwing vegetables. Lynette Reini-Grandell allowed me to read from the first chapter in progress on KFAI-AM in Minneapolis.

Sarah, Simon, and Lucy Kaplan showed me what the *haimish*ness of Rabbi Friedman's house looks like in others.

So many friends helped me get this book done in so many ways that to list them and their contributions would minimize them all in the nothingness of further fine print. You know who you are and so do I, and I will thank you each in a better way.

Finally, this book is a forever *l'chaim* to Daisy Orenstein Okazaki and commemorates the memory of Lucius Pollack (1989-2003), son of Geoffrey and Sharon Pollack, *alev v'shalom*. Lucius, we'll all be seeing you in a better place.

CONTENTS

1

UNCLE TOM JEW

Ain't no one to place the blame
It's too smart to have a name.
—Southern slave spiritual

In the seconds between shoving my third and fourth White Castle–sized pork sandwich down my throat, I yelled across the lavishly appointed basement toward my host. He and his wife had invited fifty Twin Cities WASPs, and me, to watch Mike Tyson's pay-per-view, main-event boxing match in Las Vegas against heavyweight Frans Botha on their wide-screen television.

I was more interested in the undercard fight for the junior cruiserweight championship belt between the Brooklyn-born Ethiopian Jew Zab Judah and Wilfredo Negron.

"Hey, Jim, call me when the Hebe's fight comes on," I said from the kitchen. I then turned toward the Minnesota crowd waiting with empty buns on paper plates for their own turns at the buffet.

"Zab Judah is the only Yid champ left!" I said loudly to no one in particular but to everybody specifically. "Naturally, they'll never make the Hebe the headline bout, the Nazi bastards!"

Someone shoved a Budweiser into my hand, my fourth of the night. "Well, I usually don't do this," I said, laughing, as I popped the top. "I'm not from a drinking people, you know. It's right there in the Old Testament, Genesis, Chapter Four in the book of Shmeckel: 'And God gave Moses the bong, and it was good. And He said if thou shalt spill the bong water on the carpet, it shalt reek for seven genera- tions . . .' "

The kitchen exploded. "I missed that one in Sunday school," a blond woman said, laughing the hardest.

As usual, I was enticed by her Crest smile, the way she laughed at my jokes like they, or I, were deeper than I was letting on. The delicate little gold cross on a chain hung over her turtleneck, indicating she was as forbidden to me as I was to her.

This was my kind of woman. When asked why I went out only with non-Jewish women, I had a stock reply that further outraged or cracked up most any audience I was able to gather.

"Jewish women *hate* me," I said that night, as I often did. "I think I remind them of their annoying Uncle Morty, the schmuck at the Seder table with the stupid hundred-year-old Borscht Belt jokes. They want lawyers from Plymouth, not writers living in the middle of the city. As Abbie Hoffman said, 'You go for the gelt or you go for broke.' They don't want to go for broke."

In my more self-righteous moments I likened myself to an Abbie Hoffman–troublemaking Jew. I hadn't gone what I considered the easy route of suburban-bred Twin Cities Jew. I wasn't a lawyer or orthodon- tist trained at the University of Minnesota. I hadn't been a member of Sigma Alpha Mu, the Jewish fraternity known as the Sammies. My gen- eration of Minneapolis Jews had almost all gone for the gelt, eventually ending up in a house with 2.3 kids in Twin Cities' suburban gilded ghetto.

I viewed them from afar as judgmental ignorants. Of course, I was the one judging, projecting my own despair and need to belong back at them. I saw how they took care of each other when someone died: the shiva, the food, the communal tears. I wondered narcissistically who would mourn me, thinking of an old Yiddish joke about a Jew so bad no one could find a eulogist. Finally, a rabbi volunteered, offering up the words: "His uncle was worse." Though I pretended not to care, I did.

Outwardly, at least, I wanted to emulate my heroic Jewish outlaws; I wanted to join the spirit of what people like the ones mystery writer Kinky Friedman and founder of a country and western band called the Texas Jewboys enumerated.

From Moses, Friedman said in the *Forward,* "a long line of Jewish troublemakers followed—Baruch Spinoza, Karl Marx, Groucho Marx, Lenny Bruce, Abbie Hoffman—who were spiritual beacons in a [gentile] world. "These among other *lantzman,*" Friedman continued, also served as lighthouses for frightened Jews who for millennia "shun trouble, avoid at all cost confrontations . . . we who look in our mirrors [and] are mildly surprised that we're still here."

Now, that was me. I felt like an obsolete pinball machine whose spare parts hadn't been made. I was also a self-deluded fool. Standing here, outraging my audience, I was no Jewish outlaw like Abbie, throwing bills to the floor of the Stock Exchange. At best I was a Vegas lounge act.

Unconsciously, I threw in a joke to the crowd in the kitchen, a Henny Youngman one-liner:

"Why do Jewish husbands always die before Jewish wives?" I asked.

"Because they *want* to."

The room erupted and I reached for another beer.

I was shticking like Milton Berle on crystal meth, using a speed rap I'd developed at college parties to get a group of gentile women to encircle me. If they were laughing at my rap here, I figured, they couldn't ogle the sensitive guitar player singing Grateful Dead tunes in the living room. *Shagetz* (non-Jewish) musicians always had it easier than Jewish men in getting the girls. I'd joke in the kitchen, where everybody had to pass by me on the way to beer and food. In Minneapolis—at concerts, ball games, dinner parties, the theater during intermission, walking along the street, or standing in a virtual stranger's kitchen eating *trayf* (nonkosher food)—I delighted in outraging the gentiles. I was engaged in shtetl *shpritzing,* Jewish jazz.

Did my non-Jewish friends perchance want to see my horns, I'd ask, or the yellow stripe running down my back? And gee, I'd throw in, sorry about killing your Lord and all that, it was a party, things got out of hand, he didn't chip in for the Last Supper's tip. Before launching into my full-blown anti-Jewish joke parade, I half insulted them by slightly altering some of Henny Youngman's Polish jokes.

"Did you hear about the guy who was half Swedish and half Jewish?

"He's the janitor of a building, but he *owns* it."

"Shpritzing?" the blonde at the party asked.

"Surrounded by other Jewish wise guys, usually at a diner or deli, you just shoot out jokes as fast as you can and everybody tries to top you," I said, staring at her. "When they were young, Lenny Bruce (né Leonard Schneider), Rodney Dangerfield (né Jacob Cohen), Jerry Lewis (né Joseph Levitch), and whatever Jewish comic was in town shoehorned themselves into a booth in a Brooklyn diner and *shpritzed* faster than Chuck Yeager flew. *Shpritzing* was the Jewish right stuff. Henny Youngman claimed that Jerry Lewis even *shtupped* a woman in the candy store's phone booth without missing the beat of his jokes. Now Lenny, there was a Jew considered a *shanda fur di goyim.*"

Nobody asked what *shtupping* was, but the blond woman said, "I heard of Lenny Bruce, he was in that R.E.M. song about the end of the world. What is a . . . *shalen goy* . . . ?"

"Let's see," I said, thinking of an example. "Woody Allen getting arrested for molesting or at least marrying his child is a *shanda fur di goyim.*"

"I don't understand," she of the golden, dangling crucifix said.

"Let's put it this way," I said. "When Abbie Hoffman was screaming

at the inept Judge Julius Hoffman at his infamous Chicago Seven con-
spiracy trial . . ."

"I studied that in college," she said. "A lot of people think that was
the most important trial of the century."

I *liked* this shiksa. She knew Lenny Bruce and Abbie Hoffman, al-
beit through Michael Stipe songs and college history texts. "Yeah," I
said, "well, Abbie screamed in court to the judge, 'You're a disgrace to
the Jews in front of America! You're a *shanda fur di goyim!' A shanda fur
di goyim* is the worst thing one Jew can say to a Jew—it means you're
such a rat bastard that you make all Jews look bad in front of the
goyim." They all laughed. Christ, the gentiles loved being called goyim
to their faces by a crazy Jew.

How could I make such a spectacle of myself and talk such trash, be
such an unmitigated ass, after all that had happened, I wondered
briefly, a suddenly conscious current of self-loathing making me want
to crawl out of my skin. But I quickly repressed the noxious feeling
that mocked who I had become during the last two decades—a buffoon who despised who he was and where he'd come from.

Even when I was still a kosher-keeping and religious youth, studying Hebrew and ancient Aramaic harder than anyone I knew, I'd tried
to get away from my ancestry and be just an American kid, as in the
sit-com fantasies of gentile life, ironically almost always written by
first-generation Jews, peopled by kids who couldn't fall asleep on
Christmas night.

As split inside as Cain and Abel, I'd had plans to be a rabbi, yet I'd
always wanted to fit in, to assimilate. I didn't want to be just a "normal" kid but rather a brave outlaw. So I was the bookie for my tenth-
grade class, taking bets in the lunchroom on Friday for that Sunday's
game before heading home to prepare for Shabbos.

I'd totaled four cars, been arrested for big-ticket shoplifting at fourteen, had my license suspended at seventeen by altering it to make it

look, I thought, as if I were old enough to drink. The judge gave me only the mandatory one-month suspension when I told him I needed to get to the synagogue every Saturday to teach religion, which was actually *true*. During those four weeks, I simply hitchhiked down Minneapolis's busiest thoroughfare in my suit, John Dillinger with a tallis bag instead of a tommy gun in hand.

At school I wrestled and played freshman hockey, punching and flipping gentiles on their backs to middlin' success, but at least proving I was no weakling Jew. At forty, I hadn't known or cared for decades where my Phi Beta Kappa key was, but my framed certificate for being the 104-pound wrestling champion of my seventh-grade class followed me everywhere I lived.

Only later did I realize that my need to "prove" myself was about asserting my masculinity. I felt that as a Jew my manhood was always in question. Just as most Jewish women are revolted by the stereotype of the JAP, I was repulsed by perceptions of the weak, pale yeshiva boys Isaac Babel wrote of, "studying in fright in the shtetl, with spectacles on [their] nose and autumn in their heart."

Even when I'd believed, I'd often pulled against my Hebraic side in the great assimilation tug-of-war. At Jewish summer camp, I always had a great time with the kids who hated being there in the first place and enjoyed breaking all the rules in a race to see who could get thrown out of camp first. (I never did, but I wanted to. I imagined I would walk out of camp like Chuck Connors at the beginning of *Branded*.)

I'd wear a tallis, a prayer shawl, if I had to go to synagogue. It looked like a funky scarf. But as for putting on and wearing tefillin, the black prayer-box phylacteries bound at the head and arm? *Kish mir in tuchus*. Kiss my ass. The last time I'd donned the ridiculous-looking straps had been at camp. There, I remembered my overwhelming thought each day as I prayed, a fourteen-year-old bound into these goofy straps and boxes on my arm and atop my head: *I'm glad nobody at school can see this.*

Even now, when I'd make an occasional and strained effort at being a good Jew, I wouldn't put on tefillin. The idea of wearing as much an image of anti-Semitic caricatures of Jews over the centuries as they were religious objects, still made me shiver. When I got up at dawn and sat next to my father or mother at the synagogue to hear them say kaddish for my grandparents on the anniversary of their deaths, I wouldn't join my father in putting on the straps. I was there only to convey to my parents the message, *When the time comes, I'll do this for you too*.

The last half dozen years of attempted assimilation since my divorce had been the worst. Some people learn their life lessons by running into a brick wall once before learning to go around; I often needed to crash headlong into the stones one hundred times before I figured out what was wrong. During those moments, I never thought of the very old joke I could have used: Why are you hitting yourself on the head with a board over and over? Because it feels so good when I stop.

"I don't want to miss the Hebe," I reminded some strangers in the kitchen.

My own offensiveness—and what it said about my lack of self-respect—was more than counterbalanced by the flattering attention of an all-gentile, all-American crowd laughing at the outrageous goofy Jew playing the shtetl idiot for their amusement. Still soaking in the laughter, I continued to hang in back where the cohost Celeste was ladling shredded pork from a steaming silver kettle into mini–Wonder Bread buns.

"Didn't eat today, Neal? Would you like another?" she asked, but before I could say yes, she grew stricken. "Oh, God. I'm *so* sorry. *Pork*. I should have had another dish!"

I wondered if she even would have known my religion if I hadn't made such a spectacle of myself. "Don't be silly, I'm a pork slut," I responded, piling my paper plate high.

"I didn't know Jews could eat pork," said Celeste as she watched me snarf my fifth sandwich in one bite. "Don't you go to hell? No, wait—Jews don't believe in hell, right?"

"Anybody Catholic here?" I asked, an equal-opportunity mocker. A few hands in the kitchen went up. "I think priests should get married so they'd *really* know what hell is."

Rim shot. I felt a brief shiver of hating myself, but everyone was laughing again. And then the tug from the other side, the long-ago-educated-in-Judaism side. "Jews have hell," I said defensively. "It's called Gehenna. And actually, Celeste," I said, pork juice dribbling out of my mouth, "I didn't taste pig until I was twenty-one. I almost became a rabbi."

"You? I don't believe it."

"No shit. Me a rabbi. Sagely telling everybody what to do. Like they need any help. My sermons every week would have been the same nine-word history of the tribe: 'They tried to kill us; we won; let's eat.' "

I was a Jewish Uncle Tom. And for almost two decades, I'd been busy reinventing myself, reinforcing the worst stereotypes of Jews and the community. I'd once taken that community to my heart like a precious birthright but then had tossed away like worthless fool's gold.

My Judaism hadn't retreated; it had evaporated.

2

THE *SHANDA*

What have I in common with Jews? I have hardly anything in common with myself.

—Franz Kafka, *Diaries*

Celeste still looked shocked at the notion of my almost becoming a rabbi. I good-naturedly nudged her.

"I'd have become a priest, but I can't drink that early."

"No, really," she said, avoiding my dodge. "You were going to become a rabbi?"

"I was knockin' on heaven's door my senior year in college when I realized I believed in heaven and God only half the time. I'd have become what I always loathed—one of those self-righteous rabbis who'd tormented me for the previous fifteen years," I said.

"God, I'm stunned," she said. "I mean, I've only met you a few times but, um, I always thought you were just, pardon me for saying . . . a *clown*. Like that's what you wanted to be. Not that there's anything *wrong* with that," she said, recovering nicely.

"Like Emmett Kelly the clown?" I asked.

"That was his *act*," she said.

"Well, you never saw him in public out of his makeup—and this is *my* public act," I said, smiling. "In Yiddish, it's called shtick. This is my shtick."

I referenced the Lutheran theologian Kierkegaard, my favorite anti-Semitic philosopher, and told her his retelling of the mythological story about a guy to whom the gods offered any wish. "Will you have youth, or power, or a long life, or the most beautiful maiden, or any of the glories? Choose, but only one," I recited.

"So what did he pick?" Celeste asked.

"I choose this one thing," I quoted the beneficiary, "that I may always have the laugh on my side."

"So you decided to play a full-time clown instead of a half-believing rabbi?" Celeste said, needling me as she tried to figure out the equation.

"Hey, the hours are better. The only thing I have in common with Jews is that I don't like to work on Saturdays."

The kitchen crowd had gathered around me again as I continued to shtick in earnest, and I didn't hear Jim yell to me from the front of the room when Zab Judah was heading from his dressing room to the ring, led by his entourage of black Jewish friends and family. It would have been a rare and happy sight for me to see a Jewish boxing champion. Yiddishkeit. Lore.

In my role as a Jewish Uncle Tom, I also told the usual, sickest, most outrageous Jewish jokes I knew to non-Jewish friends—my only friends. I told *those* jokes, the ones only Jews supposedly can tell, but never in a roomful of non-Jews, even if they were getting paid for it.

"Sam, I'm so sorry, I heard your factory burned down last Tuesday!

"Shut up you idiot, it's *next* Tuesday!"

And the worst:

"Why do Jews have such long noses?"

"Because air is free."

Or:

"How many Jews can you fit in a Volkswagen?"

"47,293. Two in front, two in back, and 47,289 in the ashtray."

I wanted to belong.

I then heard Jim's voice cutting through the din of the crowd and the giant-sized television. The host was a swell-hearted, brainy guy who I knew didn't harbor a single racist or anti-Semitic thought. But now he'd been pushed and revved by an earlier riff of mine about Jewish boxers and my continuing blasphemous references to my people.

"Hey, Neal!" he yelled over fifty gentile heads to tell me the outcome of the fight. "The Hebe won!"

He suddenly looked as horrified as his wife when she offered me a pork sandwich. He waxed relieved when I laughed louder than anyone in the room.

My shtick seemed to bring out the worst in people. After I riffed to a woman with the familiar sorry-to-have-killed-your-Lord routine, she nodded her head in agreement and made a reference to "Jew people" that clanged against my ears. "Wow," she said, "that's weird. I've never said 'Jew people' before."

Only later, while reading Professor Michael Burleigh's acclaimed *The Third Reich: A New History* did I understand that I was actually *encouraging* people to be anti-Semitic. Hitler's obsessions, Burleigh wrote, "concerned an abstraction dubbed 'the Jew' rather than actual Jews."

Jew people.

A few minutes later, shortly before the Tyson bout, two familiar faces entered the basement. From my high school class, they were Bob and Judy Schwartz. She wore a diamond as big as the Ritz. He worked as a money manager and drove a convertible BMW.

Seeing them now, I shouted across the room, "What are *you* doing here? *I'm* supposed to be the only Jew here!"

Bob laughed, not sure what the joke was.

"Don't be a *shanda fur di goyim!*" I yelled, wishing I could call out instead to everyone else in the room. *Hey goyim, I'm a goy! Don't think of me that way, like the Schwartzes! I'm not with them! I'm not a* shanda fur di goyim! They were the kind of Jews I didn't want to be associated with. I thought their material life was gaudy, but deep down I wanted to be part of a community, invited to bar mitzvahs, brises, shivas, and be proud of my birthright.

I couldn't have been more insulting to the Schwartzes if I'd called Bob a schmuck on a stick. But neither knew Yiddish, I remembered from their short stints in elementary Hebrew school. And they certainly didn't possess a *Yiddishe hartz,* the true soul of Judaism that surrounded the warm, open, and sensitive to injustice anywhere. They were the kind of Jews my age who lived in houses apportioned to Monopoly game hotel size and seemed to work in what they referred to as "financial services." The kind I knew called African Americans *"schvartzes,"* Yiddish just this side of "nigger"; when they ran into me with a date (I'd later hear) they had called her a "shiksa," an epithet only a bit up from the curb from "whore."

They saw themselves as holy Jews, but they had never embraced any sense of Yiddishkeit, the essence of the religion beyond their prayers, encompassing every tale that swelled Jews' hearts with pride, from Moses receiving the Torah, to Judah Maccabee battling the Romans, to Sandy Koufax, the Los Angeles Dodger who sat out the first game of the 1965 World Series right here in Minneapolis because it was Yom Kippur.

All that had eluded the Schwartzes, in their inexorable trek to the suburbs. How else to explain their lack of Yiddishkeit than their embracing the new, often gaudier Jewish suburbs that had sprung outward from my own after all my friends and I had gone over the wall the first second it was possible? I had escaped Minneapolis's shtetl, specifically to study back east with Rabbi Jacob Neusner, the Orthodox professor, because he was—and still is—considered the country's most brilliant Jewish academic scholar. From there, went my announced plan to my family, I was going to Hebrew Union College, in Cincinnati, where I'd be ordained myself, then return and try and make these Jews from my hometown finally *think,* to try and show that having a *Yiddishe kopf* meant more than knowing where to get it wholesale.

Besides being a *shanda fur di goyim*, one could be a *shanda fur di mishpocha*—a scandal within a family, where the shame stayed buried and secret. Worse, one could be a *shanda fur di shtetl*, a disgrace within the American suburb, who was snubbed and gossiped about inside the modern Jewish village. The disgraced was seriously sanctioned in the community, but at least the scandal was *kept* in the community. But the worst thing remained the *shanda fur di goyim*—a Jew who behaved so badly that he reflected scandalously on all Jews to all gentiles.

Michael Milken and Ivan Boesky were *shanda fur di goyim*, and before gangster chic hit, so were Meyer Lansky and Bugsy Siegel. And now, though I projected it onto the Schwartzes, so was I.

Calling them a *shanda fur di goyim* was a terrible thing to say to the Schwartzes, and I felt a wave of physical revulsion at my own rudeness. Thank God they were so ignorant of Yiddishkeit. Still, my enmity was pretty obvious.

Perhaps it was out of pure jealousy that I didn't want to be associated with the Bob and Judy Schwartzes of Minneapolis. They weren't torn as I was between the gentile world and the Jews; they seemed to feel no painful tug. True, I thought they were as phony as paste pearls, conspicuously consuming *shandas*, but how was it that they were able to become Americans in a way I never could and still retain their status as "good Jews"?

My stomach suddenly churning, I waved my host over to tell him I had to leave before the main event. Jim came up with a broad Irish smile to shake my hand good-bye. "Thanks, Neal, you get enough to eat?" he asked.

Unable to resist, I said, "Jew get enough to eat?"

Jim looked upset, thinking he'd angered me earlier, and whispered into my ear, "I'm sorry about calling Zab Judah a Hebe. I don't know where that came from. I've never used that word in my life."

"*I* know where that came from," I said, waving off his remorse. "*I* put that word in your mouth. *I* made you say it."

It was true, of course. At the same time, paradoxically, I stopped blaming myself and was angrily pulled the other way to my buried Jewish side.

A goy bleibt a goy, I thought ungenerously about Jim. "Once a gentile, always a gentile," goes the Yiddish idiom. Scratch any non-Jew and you'll probably find an anti-Semite-in-waiting. Remember how civilized things were in Germany in 1932 and Spain in 1491?

I left the house wordlessly, my stomach growing queasy.

My father's entire family had been machine-gunned in Russia and buried in pits, most still alive, by Hitler's advancing *Einsatzgruppen,* or death squads. Not that I didn't *care* about that stuff: to the contrary, I was borderline obsessed. I had literally hundreds of books dealing with every aspect of the Third Reich, from the Final Solution to irrelevant minutiae concerning whether Hitler's niece slept with the führer and then committed suicide, to the dimensions of a can of Zyklon B, the gas dropped in the concentration camp "showers."

No longer did I chant Torah in front of a congregation I loved as I'd done scores of times growing up. Instead, alone, I now studied with rage how Franklin Roosevelt ensured the slaughter of millions of Eastern European Jews, first by not allowing them to immigrate to the United States, then by refusing to bomb the train lines that ran directly into Auschwitz, even though American planes were firebombing other train tracks only a few miles away.

I didn't have anyone Jewish I respected to talk to about it, even if I'd wanted to.

From an underground press, I'd bought a book called *The Einsatzgruppen Reports,* composed entirely of official missives sent by the German death squads in Russia back to the home office in Berlin. Since my grandfather's family was from Karlin, near Pinsk, I thought there might be a clue inside its shabby covers showing when the deed actually occurred.

> The Chief of the Security Police   Berlin, August 20, 1941
> Operational Situation Report USSR No. 58, Executive Activity
> August 12–13, 1941
> *Instigation and incitements by the Jews continue to increase. A member of the militia was shot dead from an ambush near Pinsk. As a reprisal, 4,500 Jews were liquidated.*

I grew enraged for hours almost every time I read this bloodless description of ongoing genocide. I made my obsession a joke, like I was a Civil War reenactor or member of the Flat Earth Society. When friends came to my apartment and inspected my video collection, they'd ask why I had the entire Nuremburg trials on tape, and I'd laugh about how they should rename the History Channel, my favorite station, the Hitler Channel. I told them that whenever I was depressed, I'd watch some Nazis get hanged, and I'd perk right up.

My fascination was perverse. I had no idea what I got out of this singularly horrible thing in Judaism—while seeking none of its joy. Looking back, I see that it was my too self-conscious repudiation of who I was. Inspecting my bookshelves, friends would ask why I had such seminal texts on the war against Jewry as Robert Jay Lifton's *Nazi Doctors,* Daniel Jonah Goldhagen's *Hitler's Willing Executioners,* and Hannah Arendt's *Eichmann in Jerusalem* atop a collection of virulently anti-Semitic literature I'd collected over the years since I'd dropped out of Judaism. Or why did I have a framed page from *Harper's* magazine of its 1882 serialization of a Charles Dickens novel dominated by a woodcut captioned "Oliver Twist and Fagin the Jew"?

"I don't know," I'd say. Silently, I'd think of the old comic strip "Pogo" and his famous line, "We have met the enemy—and he is us." Only he, I'd now come to know, was me.

No matter which side pulled harder in my personal tug-of-war between Jew and assimilated American, I was now finally sure of one thing—I was about to be pulled into the mud pit in the middle where the losers end up.

As soon as I left Jim and the boxing behind, I slunk out the door and went immediately into a shame spiral that seemed to dissolve my spine and knock me off my feet. Gathering my balance, I walked into the rain, away from my car, and toward the Mississippi River. I sat on the bank, the mud seeping through my blue jeans.

And then it hit me; just as I was gathering enough strength to lift myself out of my own humiliation and self-pity, the beer and pork sandwiches came up violently, angrily. I kept heaving until there was nothing left, and then again and again, until I was unable to stop gasping and began praying to a God I hadn't believed in for decades to let me catch my breath.

One piece of the bullshit I'd flung that night had been true. I *had* come within an electron of becoming a rabbi.

At the exact moment I was supposed to begin at Hebrew Union College, in Cincinnati, for five years of rabbinical training, I instead began work at *Newsweek* on Fiftieth and Madison, where the only guaranteed things were I'd see a lot more as a twenty-one-year-old reporter with a snappy-looking press pass than as a freshman rabbi. Every single Jewish Sabbath I'd be up all Friday night until five the next morning, then return to the office after a few hours of sleep in case the world blew up on Saturday, the day the magazine closed.

Though some might have been proud, my big-city job meant nothing to my parents, who were less than wowed that they could now tell their neighbors to pick up a magazine in St. Louis Park with an article I'd written in New York. Having grown up with their values, *I* wasn't that proud either.

I'd denied my family their *yichus,* the grandest honor a family could have. *Yichus* had nothing to do with money, but with a familial line of scholarship. You couldn't buy *yichus,* you had to earn it. Ten generations of a family line dedicated to scholarship was more valuable than riches. Indeed, in both the shtetl and America, one of the greatest honors a rich man can achieve is supporting a son-in-law so he won't have to work to provide a living for his daughter and grandchildren. Such acts were considered transfusions of *yichus.*

There would be no *yichus* for my family.

By my senior year, my faith had wavered. Breaking out from my xenophobic hometown shtetl with the freedom to assimilate, I learned about existentialism from atheist professors far smarter than any rabbi back home. I started to wonder why I was any more "chosen" than gentiles, whom for the first time I now counted as best friends.

At college my vistas had expanded. I was surrounded by new ideas of goyim I hadn't been exposed to in my Minnesota shtetl, like Kierkegaard's "The Christianity of Us Men," the meditations of St. Thomas Aquinas, and nations of people; there were homecoming queens named Muffin and roommates with the middle name Xavier. I figured I'd either have to be an idiot or be made of sterner stuff than I was not to begin to question.

By the time I was ready to graduate, I believed only about half the time that God existed and had "chosen" the Jews. If I followed through with my plans, I would become exactly what I'd always loathed: a rabbinic hypocrite. A phony, standing up on the bimah under the Ten Commandments, telling people right from wrong when I myself hadn't a clue.

So I turned a 180 on my ambitions, as screechily as Gene Hackman famously pursuing *something* in *The French Connection*'s bang-'em-up New York chase sequence, and aimed for a fabulous career in the big metropolis I'd seen only as an eleven-year-old.

Then, eight years later I walked into a terrible mugging in which I was pounded with fists, kicked several times, and learned what taxi wheels going sixty miles an hour sounded like from ear level in the street. Looking back, though, was my own sense of weenieness, the Jewish schlub incarnate. It was right there in the police report: "Victim tried to run away but tripped over his own cowboy boots." What kind of man *was* I? Humiliated by my own weakness, I decided to come back home to Flyoverland. Familiarity and safety had drawn me to the place I'd left. "Home is the place," Robert Frost knew, "where they have to take you in."

Now, years after having moved back to my hometown, spiritual erosion had taken care of whatever remained of my belief, like a beautiful shoreline washed away because it had been untended for too many years. Projecting my own rage as a failed person, unable to find a place in the Jewish community, I turned into that judgmental jerk against my own people. Unable to monitor my own spiritual growth, I blamed others, outsiders, who were Jews like me.

As for the children I'd always loved teaching at Saturday school and tutoring one-on-one for their bar or bat mitzvahs? And the father I always knew I wanted to be?

I felt totally alone. If one's shtick falls in a forest and no one hears it . . .

I pulled up the sleeve of my jacket to check my Alfred E. Newman watch the college students I taught for a semester every two years loved to pass around, saying the kitsch was so *me*. I took off the idiotic timepiece and chucked it into the Mississippi. I was so tired of being *me*.

Suddenly, another wave of nausea keeled me over onto all fours. I was a *shanda fur mir,* a scandal to me. By exiling myself from my own tribe and lusting to be anyone, *anything* else at all, I'd in fact become nothing.

3

A STRANGER ON A PLANE

Weeks later, I was on a plane from Los Angeles to Minneapolis. I sat down next to a Hasidic rabbi, not knowing at the time that in talking to him I would have one of the most mind-quaking revelations of my life. I didn't see God, but I began, for the first time in memory, to see myself. After a few minutes of idle conversation about the weather—we both lived in the Twin Cities—he began gently quizzing me about how I practiced my Judaism. *Funny, I'd never told him I'd been born Jewish.*

"Do you wear tefillin?" he asked. It had been decades since I'd put on the prayer phylacteries that contained inscriptions from the Torah inside small boxes that are placed on the head and arm and bound with straps in a precise ritual every morning.

"No," I said.

"Do you belong to a shul?" he continued.

"I love Judaism," I said, trying to stick a pin in the ass of one more rabbi who'd crossed my path, "it's Jews I can't stand."

He wasn't offended—and offered what seemed a non sequitur.

"The ultimate question," he responded, "is can Jews get along?"

19

"And?" I asked.

"No," said Rabbi Manis Friedman, smiling, a gray beard flowing down his chest.

"People often tell me I'm the most *ethnic,* least *Jewish* Jew they've ever met," I said to the Hasid, a member of the sect of the ultra-Orthodox who embarrass so many mainstream Jews.

They were a *shanda fur di goyim* for refusing to make any concessions in their beliefs about modern America or assimilating. People said they smelled, made love through a hole in a sheet, would cheat a gentile in business like Shylock, and never mowed their lawns, bringing down neighbors' property values. This was not good for the shtetl, even if the village was Shaker Heights or Scarsdale.

Rabbi Friedman was returning from a trip to South Africa, a fifty-six-year-old father of fourteen, so jet-lagged and exhausted that the last thing he probably needed were wisecracks from such an exaggerated form of assimilated, self-loathing Jew as me.

I already knew that for all my cultural Jewishness, memorization of Nazi troop movements, and once-upon-a-time ability to read and take to heart the Torah, my current habit of making fun of myself and other Jews didn't necessarily make me a good Jew. So *what,* I wondered, did it make me? And this is what I started to ask the rabbi—in order to squelch the boredom of the flight, in part because, deep down, I thought he might have the answers to my paradox, the pull between who I was and who I once thought I wanted to be but couldn't.

I asked him in vague terms about my performance before the gentiles at the boxing match not long before. By ridiculing myself as a Jew, I asked, wasn't I perhaps a shtetl-like *badchen,* the old-world jester hired by wedding parties to comically insult and shock the bride, groom, and guests as the klezmer band played on?

The notion, Rabbi Friedman said, that my making fun of Judaism the way I had watching the boxing matches, differentiating myself from the know-nothing Schwartzes, somehow elevated me to a higher plane was a fool's grandeur. "You were playing yourself for a buffoon, to be laughed *at. Not* good."

He paused. "What kind of jokes? Would they be jokes you'd be ashamed for your granddaughter or son to hear?"

"Nah," I lied. I did my Uncle Tom shtick that I'd picked up from old Jewish comics and appropriated to make gentiles laugh by proving how we Jews were indeed stereotypable goofy monkeys tied to God knows what organ-grinder.

"Were these comedians you knew happy?" Rabbi Friedman asked. "Most comedians I've met are miserable, and miserable people."

"I revered them," I said. "God sneezed, I didn't know what to say. I go to a synagogue so Reform it's closed on Saturdays," I babbled on. "Those are Henny Youngman jokes. I liked him when I was helping Henny with his autobiography. I liked how he took me back to the past, back to Jewish vaudeville. He told me who I think I was in a previous life. One day, he dropped his fork at the Friars Club and said I looked exactly like a terrible balloon twister he used to know on the Coney Island boardwalk."

"Hmmm," Rabbi Friedman said, looking disinterested. And then he paused like a professional laugh getter.

" 'I made instant coffee in a microwave oven and went back in time,' " he quoted.

"Hey," I said, "what's a Hasidic rabbi doing quoting Steven Wright?"

"Even rabbis have to keep their ears open, though not to blasphemy," he said.

"*Especially* rabbis have to keep their ears open."

Now I wanted to get serious. "So in a lot of ways I really think I *was* that Coney Island balloon twister in a previous life," I said, meaning it. As a kid I always had pictures of New York Mets and Jets players up on my wall, not Minnesota Twins or Vikings, even though I'd been to New York only once.

Rabbi Friedman looked at me impassively.

"Do the Hasidim believe in reincarnation?" I asked.

He looked at me and smiled. "*I* believe you can be reincarnated in your own lifetime."

For years I'd been unable to make the recalibrations necessary to truly become a man—a good, kind man, a mensch—with the heart and soul I had thought I'd earn through my belief in Judaism.

I had taken pride in my willingness to tip over the Monopoly board of my life and start over. It had worked when I graduated from college and went to New York instead of rabbinical school; it worked when I left New York with no prospects. In truth, there was only one event that paralyzed me, made me unable not only to change but also to keep my footing and stay where I was: I married the person I thought was my soul mate.

I'd first seen her across a room of 250 people at a Christmas party, pointed my arm in her direction, and for the only time in my life said, "I want her."

She was my final dive into total assimilation. Heather was every Jewish mother's nightmare, the woman who would make her grand-children Christian. She was the ultimate blond shiksa goddess, not just a former cheerleader for a major league team, but a former *skating* cheerleader for the Minnesota North Stars.

"America is a *shiksa* nestling under your arm whispering love love love love love!" whined Alexander Portnoy. "Skating behind the puffy red earmuffs and the fluttering yellow ringlets . . . how do they get so gorgeous, so healthy, so *blond*?"

She was no bimbo, though. Heather had a master's degree in jour-nalism and was the editor of a local environmental magazine. With her, I was finally going to be an American. I could ditch my shtick. I could stop making excuses for what I was when I was around her.

I proposed when she gave me her North Starlettes jacket with "Heather" stitched professionally above the big "N" that she wore while skating with the hockey team. We melded cultures when, for a temporary engagement ring, I gave her a vaudeville gag that Henny Youngman had given me. It was a dime soldered to the top of a Crackerjack ring—a "diamond ring," get it?

"Kid, no true lady can say no to a dime and ring."

Looking in the rear view of my life I suppose I got what I deserved in some way for my Judao-macho bullshit of picking some gentile woman out of a crowd—and then getting her. When I'm more forgiving, I think of the sixteenth century Saint Teresa's dictum that "more tears are shed for answered prayers than unanswered ones."

Only moments after the judge hitched us, I knew the marriage would never work. My father was sitting next to Heather's Catholic grandfather, telling a story about our whole family driving back home from a cousin's wedding in Chicago decades ago. Going through Wisconsin, my father continued, he'd been stopped by a state patrolman who solicted a $100 bribe to tear up the ticket. "What could I do?" my father said. "I didn't want to come back to Wisconsin, which was the law, so I paid him."

"You should have Jewed him down," her grandfather said.

And then her grandpa said it again. "You should have Jewed him down."

As the slurs clanked against my dad's ears, I saw the artery pop out of his neck and pulsate like a wrestler caught in the vise of a potentially fatal chokehold. I felt as if I were literally killing my father. I ran around the table to make sure my old man wouldn't smack the anti-Semitic fuck, even though he deserved it.

"Don't worry," my father whispered to me. "I'm not going to ruin your wedding."

I then ran back and sat back down next to Heather and said, dripping horror and the shame of bringing disrespect to my father, whose toughness I'd always wanted to emulate. Now I wanted the strength to say nothing. "Your grandfather just said the most anti-Semitic thing to my father," I told her. "Can you just go say something nice to my old man, give him a kiss or something, make him feel better?"

Instead she turned on me in a way I'd never seen her do to anyone before. Her face crumpled, like the grand beach hotel that was demolished by dynamite and collapsed at the beginning of *Atlantic City*.

For better or worse . . .

She then furiously started defending her grandfather in a fierce, loud stage whisper.

"He can't help it, he's an old man!" she spat out.

In sickness and health . . .

"He doesn't know any better . . ." she continued. "It's your fault."

I could no longer hear what she was saying. I just saw that I had married someone who was not on my side, the side of the good folk. I don't mean the *Jewish* side, but my side, *our* side.

Until death do you part . . .

I was dead.

My faith—in Judaism, in being connected to anything greater than oneself—had completely disappeared years before, back in New York. Now I'd lost faith in love itself; I had married not my soul mate, or even a stranger, but a betrayer. We were divorced within eighteen months.

What replaced whatever vestiges of faith I had in *anything* was a dank loneliness. It wasn't the existential angst kind of loneliness, sitting in a room by oneself, bricked off from humanity. Nor was it a loneliness based on having *no* connection to life. Rather, it was the loneliness of realizing that all the connections I counted on to help get me through the night weren't real. I'd lived my whole existence to feel bonded and connected to *something*.

Now I had long lost my need, ability, and desire to connect to the Jewish community. Gone were the ties to my family, both nuclear and *mishpocha* (extended family). I loved my parents and siblings, but I was rarely invited to anything anymore not because I had married a gentile, but because I simply wasn't around or interested. I'd also lost touch with most of my New York friends, partly because of the shame I still felt over the way I'd left, partly because everyone just seemed to move in their own directions.

And then came my wife, my soul mate, my *bashert* (fated love), the woman I'd connect with forever in the world, complete with white picket fence, Little League games, and the PTA. I plummeted into the loneliness and despair, as Bruce Springsteen sang, of a man "who's living in his own skin / but can't stand the company."

It wasn't the loneliness of *nobody* being there. It was the isolation of realizing that what you thought you were connected to is gone. It is the loneliness that means you can't trust yourself, or anybody else. During summer breaks in college I'd worked as an orderly in a Minneapolis hospital and couldn't help but notice as I stocked rooms with supplies that no matter how many loved ones surrounded your bed and held your hand, you truly died alone. Now it felt that this was also the truth of how one lived.

4

THE FIFTH SON AT THE SEDER TABLE (WHO NO LONGER SHOWS UP)

I'd met Rabbi Friedman on a plane after a soul-numbing week spent interviewing Hollywood flavors of the day for what I'd come to realize would be a vapid magazine article about a nonexistent trend. Before we began discussing theology, I played what I thought would be a trick. I was wearing the de rigueur Los Angeles show business uniform of black jeans, black cowboy boots, and black silk jacket that screamed, "Come back to the pool at the Chateau Marmont, *bubbelah*. I've got your next Oscar in my briefcase."

When I had boarded the plane and spotted the Hasid by his clothes, his face hidden by his newspaper, I decided to do a little shtick and surprise the stranger. I went up the aisle, leaned forward, and asked, *"Tsee iz der Ort fahr-noomen?"* (Is this seat taken?)

The Hasid looked up, smiling, expecting from my words to see one of his own—the group is the only one in the world to speak Yiddish in daily conversation. Instead, he spied me in my Hollywood duds, a Walkman around my neck leaking the Ramones' "Bonzo Goes to Bitburg."

"Nissan ben Mordechai," I said, putting out my hand, using my Yiddish name.

I then looked more closely at his face and dropped my hand in shock. "Rabbi Friedman?!" I said. "Neal Karlen. Do you remember?"

When I was ten, my synagogue sent our youth group to a mansion in St. Paul used by the Lubavitch, where a young Rabbi Friedman, then able to grow only a tiny goatee, had led us in weekends of singing and dancing. When I was thirty and a reporter for *Rolling Stone*, I'd broken the story that he'd converted Bob Dylan away from his decade as a haranguing born-again Christian and back to his original status as a Jew.

Dylan was a source of pride for Jewish men sick of being typecast as whining, mama's boys always eager to run from a fight. If they were young rabbis, they'd put references in their sermons to Dylan's "Like a Rolling Stone," considered the most important rock single in history, for its Jewish theme of a lost home and diaspora. If they were ten at Jewish summer camp, like me, they memorized "The Times They Are a Changin' " and recited it during services from the wooden platform overlooking the lake.

In the early 1980s, word was that Dylan had gone insane. He was considered the voice of his generation, the only songwriter ever nominated for the Nobel Prize in literature, so madness was the only explanation for his fundamentalist Christian concerts. They were pathetic affairs in half-filled auditoriums populated with old-time nostalgics booing. He'd responded with fire and brimstone and Jerry Falwell–like rants from the stage about Christ.

For Jewish men of the postwar generation for whom he was a prophet of revolution who had gone to Hebrew school and been bar mitzvahed just like them, it had been as if Sandy Koufax had converted to, well, evangelical Christianity.

And then a decade letter, around 1990, he'd been converted back to the tribe by Rabbi Manis Friedman of St. Paul, whose picture and full beard ran as big as Dylan's in the *Rolling Stone* article describing what had happened.

"Just please don't call me Bob Dylan's rabbi. People camp out on my doorstep, reporters. If he showed up and saw me . . ."

I'd heard a rumor transmitted to me from someone who heard it in the Minneapolis Jewish Community Center steam room. "Is it true, Rabbi Friedman," I'd asked when I interviewed him, "that Dylan showed up unannounced last year at your house on Seder night wearing leather and motorcycle boots?"

He paused, the kind of pause I knew as a reporter meant yes. "No comment, next question."

"I won't mention it," I said.

"I didn't say anything," he retorted.

I'd heard another piece of skinny at the Jewish Community Center. "Is it true he's now wearing tefillin?"

"Off the record?"

"Shoot."

"Dylan lays tefillin."

I didn't mention this tidbit to my editor or that a woebegone Dylan showed up for Passover Seder at the Friedmans'. The first because I hadn't gotten him definitely to say yes, though I knew it was true, and the second because I knew that even if he became the only rabbi ever to get his picture in *Rolling Stone,* the word *tefillin* would never make it. I kept mum also because like most Jewish men of a certain age I loved Bob Dylan and just didn't want to violate him. To nice Jewish boys everywhere, Dylan stood for all the possibilities of rebellion, and that was more important to me than any story.

"You're still the only Hasidic rabbi to have his picture in *Rolling Stone,*" I told him, and he smiled mischievously. It had indeed been a remarkable and unique interview.

"Dylan is a good family man," he said. "It's the women he chooses that are the problem."

Wow. It had taken much prodding back then to get him to confirm that Dylan was back in the tribe, under his tutelage.

"Could you just please write that he got hold of a copy of my book from 'a friend of a friend'?" he'd asked.

Forgetting the double-dip scoop—that the star was a Jew again and here was the rabbi behind the conversion—I printed it like he said.

Doing so didn't exactly make me a mensch, I thought, but in the world of celebrity journalism, I figured I'd been in the neighborhood.

"Be a mensch!" I remembered my father telling me growing up, and I'd tried. "The best kind of mitzvoth are the ones you do when nobody is watching or knows, and the tzedakah [charity] you give without asking for credit or for anybody to be aware. You still need to do them, but you don't need credit. You're not looking for A's from God."

Of course, I hadn't believed in God for years when I'd done my tiny favors for Rabbi Friedman. I'd probably done them for my father.

The Hasid looked truly concerned as his eyes took in my Hollywood reporter costume. "What have you been up to?"

"I got married. I got divorced. She was a shiksa."

"Don't use that word," he said. "It's not nice. What else?"

"Nothing really. Instead of practicing Judaism, I just write about it. Did you know that the only Jewish heavyweight boxing champion ever, Max Baer, wasn't even Jewish? It was a publicity stunt. Even though he wore a Star of David on his trunks, the great Jewish trainer Ray Arcel said he once saw Baer in the showers—and he wasn't even circumcised."

Rabbi Friedman was completely uninterested. "So what other Jewish topics," he asked, "do you write about when you're not thinking about Jews who might not be Jews?"

"I got my collection of baseball cards of Jews who played in the majors on the *New York Times* op-ed page. I also wrote a long story for a New York magazine about the Jewish hot dog vendor who built Nathan's on Coney Island."

He yawned.

"And I wrote about the poor, young Jewish lawyers from CCNY who were blackballed from New York's white-shoe law firms and were hired by Thomas Dewey to get the gangsters who ran Brooklyn's Murder, Inc., the Mafia's organized hit squad. I wrote about Jews in criminal law; you know what they say—to nail a Jew, get a Jew. Roy Cohn making sure the Rosenbergs were electrocuted, all that."

I was on a tear that sounded vaguely confessional and repentant, a little *t'shuva*-like, my own personalized turn, or at least nod, toward my faded Judaism. "In books I've also written about Jews in professional baseball and the record industry. You know what they say about the music business, '*Alle Chazzanim siz geven norish, oder alle norim nit geven zingen.*' " (All cantors are fools, but not every fool can sing.)

"That's not really writing about Judaism," he said.

I looked at the Yiddish newspaper lying on the seat. "The only thing I remember about my grandfather is his reading the Yiddish *Forward*," I said, trying to change the subject. "I couldn't understand what my grandfather said while he was alive, but I've always remembered him waiting for the *Forward* to pop through his mail chute from New York every day. I'm even doing an article for the *Forward*'s English edition, just to honor him."

Rabbi Friedman seemed interested. "Really? What are you writing about?"

I paused. I knew I was only digging myself in deeper.

"Um, Jewish boxers," I responded. I couldn't stop myself. "You ever heard of Kingfish Levinsky? He fought Joe Louis and almost fainted from fear in the first round."

"I'm sure your grandfather would be very proud," Rabbi Friedman said, but I couldn't tell if he was being sarcastic.

"Actually, probably not," I said, thinking immediately of my failed marriage and the ensuing divorce. According to Jewish law, he should have declared me dead the moment I said I was marrying a non-Jew and sat shiva for me.

For some reason I felt compelled again to try and outrage him with a last piece of Henny Youngman shtick. "Why do Jewish husbands always die before Jewish wives?" I repeated from my pathetic boxing-night performance. "Because they *want* to."

"Hmm," he said, picking up another paper, *The Jewish World,* the Twin Cities' mainstream Jewish weekly announcing bar mitzvahs, deaths, and Israeli tree plantings. "Somebody should *buy* this paper," Rabbi Friedman said, changing the subject, "and tell the people the truth."

I agreed. Why not begin with the hypocrisy of Minnesota's Jewish community? One local rabbi, who had a big happy family, was arrested three times for soliciting men in a dirty-book store on Minneapolis's main downtown drag.

Another rabbi was forced to send a letter to everyone in the congregation announcing that he'd had a three-year affair with a woman he'd been converting. He wasn't resigning. And the only reason he had to go public was that *another* woman he'd been helping to convert, and had an affair with for three years, was about to bust him for dumping her.

Self-righteous bastards, those rabbis, no better than Jim and Tammy Faye Bakker or Jimmy Swaggart. As Friedman read *The Jewish World,* I picked up that morning's *Los Angeles Times.*

"Well, it all doesn't really matter," I said in conclusion. "I'm not even Jewish anymore."

Rabbi Friedman looked up at me, folded his paper, then spoke, invoking his late rebbe, Menachem Mendel Schneerson.

"One Sunday the rebbe was publicly greeting everyone and anyone who wanted to see him at his home as he always did when he was well. A wealthy man from Manhattan stepped forward when it was his turn and said, 'Rebbe, you'll be so proud of me! I've lent one of my buildings and financed an entire night school for adults who are no longer Jewish! Isn't that great?' "

Rabbi Friedman's imitation of a grandiose, self-congratulatory Jewish businessman was perfect. His narrator's voice was soft and even. "The rebbe, however, grew very angry and didn't say a word. The businessman, seeing he'd angered the rebbe, was mortified. 'What did I do wrong?' he said. 'I thought you'd be proud of me for bringing back Jews who'd disappeared.'

" 'They didn't disappear, and they never stopped being Jews,' the rebbe said," Friedman continued softly. "You go back there and tell each of them that they are as Jewish as Abraham, Isaac, and Jacob."

"Is that a true story?" I asked.

"Yes. I was there."

He no doubt was. I learned later that the rebbe chose Friedman in the 1980s to be his simultaneous translator from Yiddish into English for his weekly, ad-libbed, Castro-length talks beamed by satellite to hundreds of thousands of Lubavitch.

The Lubavitch sect of Hasidim made concessions to modernity beyond Torah study transmitted through space. They wore felt fedoras instead of the *shtroimels,* the large round hats popular among other Hasidic sects. "The *shtroimel* isn't anything Jewish, it's just what many Hasidim adopted in Poland in the eighteenth century, like the rest of the population," Friedman said.

"The rebbe felt it was important to show respect to the countries that would take us in," he said, running his hand across the down-turned brim like Sam Spade about to go out in the rain in *The Maltese Falcon.* "He studied engineering at the Sorbonne, you know, spoke eleven languages, and felt there was no need to separate us further from our host countries, especially since the *shtroimel* isn't real Yiddishkeit, any more than the fedora. Both are just ways of covering our heads, and the rebbe even instructed us to wear them with the brim down, like Americans. And you know who hates us for it? Not Americans, but other Hasidic groups, who think not wearing a *shtroimel* is sacrilege."

The rebbe, meantime, was the fifth dynastic leader of Friedman's Lubavitch sect of Hasidim. Unfortunately, Rebbe Menachem Mendel Schneerson, the son-in-law of the previous rebbe, had died almost a decade before at eighty-one after a series of strokes, without naming a successor. To many, his passing came after he'd made broad hints he himself was the Messiah.

"These have been very rough years," Rabbi Friedman said, as the Lubavitch and their late rebbe became even greater embarrassments to mainstream Judaism.

Rabbi Friedman made a living traveling the world half the year giving speeches. Sometimes he spoke on the Kabbalah to Hasidic audiences in Argentina, on other occasions on how to find the right mate to gentiles and assimilated Jews on Manhattan's Upper West Side. Often he had no idea what his topic was until he arrived at the venue. But he was always ready, it turned out, no matter how tired, even for a stranger on a plane.

"You know the idea mentioned in the Talmud about the four sons at the Passover Seder table?" Rabbi Friedman asked.

Amid the cobwebs, I hadn't lost that one; I was still at least a semi-functioning apikores. "The wise son," I began, "the wicked son, the simple son, and the son who doesn't even know enough to ask a question."

"Good. Well, the rebbe introduced an idea that was pretty radical at the time. He said there was a fifth son, the one who refuses to come to the Seder. He doesn't just forget, he won't come. Traditionally, this was the lost member of the family, the one we don't talk about anymore, the one who '*stopped* being Jewish.' "

"That's me," I said. "I'm the one who *stopped*."

"Well, the rebbe said the fifth son, the lost one," continued Friedman, "is a Jew, and he has to be considered as such. We have to reach out to him and get him to come to the Seder table. What part of him refuses to come to the Seder? His Jewish part. His Jewish soul is objecting because the Judaism that is being offered to him does not live up to his expectations. What he wants is a *better* Judaism, not *no* Judaism. The lost son is warning us that we're drifting, becoming too petty, too insular, or simply just too bland. His Jewish soul is asking us to listen."

"So I'm the fifth son at the table, the missing one?" I asked.

"I have no idea," Rabbi Friedman said.

"The fifth son doesn't like negativity," he said. "He loves joy. For most people, if they're religious, if they like God, if they're observant and pious, then they think they've also got to be serious and cautious, because around every corner lurks a potential sin. You can't live like that, it is not what God intended, and the fifth son knows this.

"The fifth son doesn't come to the Seder because he thinks it's just for Jews. He doesn't like that. 'Why do we have to separate ourselves? Why do we have to make ourselves different?' he asks. 'Why do we have to be a small minority when we could be part of the bigger world?' "

"Nobody said it was easy being chosen," I said.

"No, the fifth son is absolutely right. If God wanted us to be insulated, a little community living in our own little enclave, why would He scatter us all over the world? Why are we everywhere if we don't belong anywhere? The fifth son is right, Judaism is not just for Jews."

"So gentiles should wear yarmulkes?" I asked.

"There are parts of Judaism that are just for Jews. There are parts of the Torah that speak to the children of Israel that they should do such and such. But in the bigger picture, Torah is not only for Jews, it's the blueprint of Creation. And this is what the fifth son wants to hear."

"Particularly," Rabbi Friedman continued, "the fifth son gets upset because at the Seder we mention the verse of Jeremiah sixteen asking God to pour his wrath out on all the rebellious nations. But the fifth son doesn't want to have anything to with that. He's not like a bunch of frustrated old people who think the whole world is against you and you're going to sit there at your Seder table and vent your frustrations on the world. He doesn't want to do this. He doesn't think this is acceptable. And he's right."

"But the passage sounds pretty straightforward to me," I said.

"The fifth son is right because nobody explained that passage to him. If you look at it at face value, it seems like venting frustrations against non-Jews. That's not what the Torah is saying. It's saying we want freedom in the world. We're celebrating freedom, and freedom comes from justice. Where there's no justice, there's no freedom."

"Sounds a little like a whitewash over that chosen business," I countered.

"No," Rabbi Friedman said. "Freeing part of the world doesn't mean whitewashing, it means including everyone to the same justice that we are held to. The greatest compliment you can give to a human being is: I hold you to the same standard that I hold myself. If I don't hold you to the same standards, then I'm not treating you like a human being."

"So what are you saying?" I asked Rabbi Friedman. "That with my shtick I was really the fifth son, a Jewish Uncle Tom, which allowed me to hide the fact from myself that I was a self-loathing Jewish buffoon? I thought Hasids were famous for their laughter!"

He didn't know who Uncle Tom was, and I tensed for a real debate about whether my buffoonery was a mask for hating what I was born. "Maybe it's a mask," he said. "Probably. There's a difference between laughter coming out of real joy where people are laughing with you, and laughter that comes from just being a clown so people can laugh *at* you and what you're pretending to be."

I swallowed that and tried to watch as the plane circled for a landing.

5

HOME, ALONE

When I returned to Minnesota from New York (a decade before I sat next to Rabbi Friedman on a plane), I shut out the Jews I had known growing up. When I was twenty-nine, virtually everyone I knew was non-Jewish; living in the city; broke; in the local media, arts, or band scene; far away from the gilded suburban ghettos where the Jews I'd grown up with lived.

My old classmates lived in enormous monstrosities built in what seemed like exclusively Jewish developments. Every hidden cul-de-sac had "Cedar" in the name—Cedar Pass, Cedar Pines, Cedar Shmeckels, I'd joke. These young Jews kept moving farther out from the city, away from real life, I thought, from the real ghettos where all our grandparents had grown up poor and publicly despised.

Whatever happened to saying you grew up on the corner of Delancey? I'd say. Though I'd grown up only in a first ring suburb, St. Louis Park, where Somalis now lived, for God's sake, I sure as hell wasn't aspiring to Cedarized shtetls meant to keep out the goyim, the husbands bringing home the gelt, to keep up with the Goldsteins. Even though they took care of each other like the old-country Jews of

Delancey, I stayed away because I thought they were parochial and ex-
cluding me.

These Minneapolis Jews seemed the classic, typical brand: clannish,
paranoid about what the goyim thought, and with a predilection for
the exact right style of late-model Cadillac—the archetypal Jew canoe,
I'd said in my worst days.

Looked at one way, the Twin Cities was a remarkably tiny shtetl. In
a population of almost three million as of 1994 there were only 45,000
Jews in the two metropolitan areas, and they banded together like the
denizens of the Alamo. The sociologist and *Nation* editor Carey
McWilliams had, after all, written in 1948 that "Minneapolis is the
capital of anti-Semitism in America."

They had been farm families, mostly. Or the one Jewish family in
town, who owned the general store and tailored suits. My mother's
family, which went back seven generations, invested every cent they
had in Europe in South Dakota farmland in the late 1800s.

While between half and two-thirds of American Jews were inter-
marrying, only 25 percent of Minneapolis and St. Paul Jews were.
From the flip side, it seemed when I returned that my old Jews were
the most incestuous and gossipy group I'd ever met, replete with
parochial and unsophisticated busybodies who'd been born, raised, and
gone to school here, married someone they probably met at Hebrew
school, then never moved.

It was a demographic fact: The Twin Cities as a whole was one of
the most stagnant populations in the country, where people never
moved from where they were born. The cemented-in Jews lived
together in enclaves so tightly knit and monolithic that gentiles from
the suburb next door could be reasonably certain they were hitting
the right targets when they threw a barrage of bagels on the ice at
my high school hockey team during games. St. Louis Park, St. *Jewish*
Park, as it was called, my own old gilded ghetto, was such an easy
target.

The whole community seemed to be a suburban Sanhedrin (the

ancient Jewish court of judgment). And it seemed that I was always bumping into their representatives, old classmates now married to each other who'd ventured into urban Minneapolis for an evening. Of course I was often out with a gentile woman when I saw them—and I'd watch as their eyes went from my date's head to her toes.

While the Jewish wife usually stared my date down, the husband would most often tell me about his thriving business and ask when I was going to settle down and have kids and a house. My date or girlfriend would look at me afterward and say, "Did you see how they looked at me? It was like I was a *thing*."

"Never mind those *shmeckels*," I'd always say, lifting whoever it was into the air by the waist and kissing her, "you'll always be my shiksa goddess."

God, I hated those people, these Jews, *my* Jews. Or was it me that I hated?

"We should get together," they'd always say in parting. *What do you mean* we, *Kemo sabe?* I thought to myself.

Those Jews were a big part of the reason that my best friends growing up, all Jewish, had also gotten out of town the second they graduated high school. Eventually almost all ended up, like me, in New York or Los Angeles or cities between, and eventually married non-Jews.

Even my parents had suffered the malicious busybody wrath of the Jews I'd grown up with. Soon after my return, I ran into an acquaintance from high school who said she'd recently seen my parents at a movie. "I always thought they were divorced," she said.

I knew why. Two decades before, my mother had fled from her stay-at-home role as a Jewish doctor's wife and taken a full-time job with the local orchestra. She had to spend one night a week at the concert hall for performances, and on that evening my father went out for dinner alone at the delicatessen a couple blocks from home.

At the deli, Mrs. Goldstein, our block's leading yenta, saw him alone and asked where my mother was. My dad, a shtickmeister too, said, "She left me. She got a job, met all these fancy people, and divorced me."

Mrs. Goldstein "hmmmed" and hustled away. By the time he got home, my mother was back and on the phone with Aunt Barbara, who always had the latest skinny on the shtetl. The word was out, and it was terrible, she told my mother—she and my father, the rumor mill had begun churning, were getting divorced.

In the time it took Mrs. Goldstein to send her smoke signals to every mezuzah-bearing house in the Twin Cities, my aunt Barbara had already fielded two dozen phone calls informing her of the false news of her sister-in-law's divorce. My mother asked Barbara to call everyone back, which she did, and tell people Mrs. Goldstein was just being a Hall of Fame yenta again.

Fun rekhiles un fun soydes/ant vi sheydim, as they say in Yiddish (From gossip and from secrets/flee as if from demons). And I did. I hadn't known goddamn Jews like this in New York.

A few years after I returned to Minneapolis, I pulled into the football stadium–size parking lot after a half-hour drive into the suburbs. I saw none of the old shul's majestic stained-glass windows, which overlooked the street from high inside the sanctuary, their magnificent breadth and spectrum of colors depicting Bible stories that had so enchanted me as a child. Here, in its place, I saw a busy-looking edifice that looked like something Frank Lloyd Wright had distractedly doodled up while talking on the telephone.

Now, I could barely stand sitting in a synagogue. Yet I wanted to attend the bar mitzvah of the child of a first cousin I'd always liked.

This synagogue bore the same name as the one I'd grown up in, but everything was different. While I'd been gone, the inner-city shul where I was bar mitzvahed, read Torah, tutored, and had given teenage sermons had been sold to a Unitarian church.

As a replacement, the next generation of synagogue *machers,* politicians, and fund-raisers had built this massive, modern suburban structure. There, I imagined, the Jews from my youth raised their children with the aspirations for material acquisition with which their parents raised *them*—to go for the gelt, not go for broke.

Inside the synagogue, I looked around at everyone else looking around at everyone else. To my eyes they were comparing hats, suits, and who was sitting with whom. Reverence or prayer seemed irrelevant.

I chided myself for being so judgmental without really knowing what was going on in their heads. After all, who was *I* to judge them, with my repeated dives for decades into the deep end of assimilation?

Simple. I *blamed* them for being people whose values I self-righteously felt I couldn't support. Maybe if they turned around on the High Holidays to kiss the Torah and stopped comparing hats or suits, maybe if their perfumes weren't so overpowering or their taste so tacky, I wouldn't have been so bitter about the religion that had once defined me. Maybe, I thought, if they paid more attention to the all-important commandment of quietly and constantly giving tzedakah instead of showing off their money like the chopped liver swan in *Goodbye, Columbus,* I wouldn't dislike the Minneapolis Jews of my youth so much.

I didn't want to belong to *that* tribe where, as my father said about grandiose displays of celebration for thirteen-year-olds who'd memorized a paragraph of the Torah, "There was more bar than mitzvah."

At the old shul, my parents could be counted on to perform any of the complicated religious tasks during services, from tying the Torah to opening the ark. They both came to early-morning minyans to say kaddish for their dead parents, my father wearing the tefillin his father had given him at his bar mitzvah. They had three children bar mitzvahed there, paying for three extra years of Hebrew study, three hours every Saturday morning. As older teenagers, their children read Torah and tutored twelve-year-olds for their bar or bat mitzvahs. They paid their dues.

They belonged to the men's club and ladies' auxiliary and had their names engraved on a small plaque in the social hall of the synagogue for what they'd done to make the place succeed; the *machers* with the money had one located in the social hall where the communal kiddush (blessing over the wine) was said after Shabbos morning services. Yet apparently none of the old plaques had been transported to the new synagogue, because the people behind that brass, I figured, were mostly forgotten.

I couldn't find a community with the kind of Jewish values my parents had raised me with, and so I had decided to separate, assimilate into being just an American, like all my normal friends.

There was a price to pay, of course. I'd had to reject not only *those* Jews but also my parents who still lived among them with their eight-year-old Dodge Dart and who never understood how I could have thrown away so much studying, so much *nachas* of being a rabbi.

My father was now a late septuagenerian, and long ago he'd put all his hopes on me. He didn't want to be able to boast in the Jewish Community Center health club, like so many other fathers, about the money his children made. Rather, he wanted me to bring home the *yichus,* the special kind of familial pride linked to religious scholarship.

I was sitting, facing his back, in a fishing boat in Canada when I was twenty-five, when I told him I was going to get married to the blond Catholic I was living with in New York. Not turning around, he quietly said he wouldn't go. "I'll send you pictures," I said, but *that* wedding didn't happen. Seven years later he'd mellowed out enough to come to the wedding, to another blond Catholic. Unfortunately, it would be the worst moment of my life.

When I found my parents inside, I asked my father about the missing family plaque, and he just hunched his shoulders and raised his palms. Were they at least still letting him sing the haftarah portion that followed the Torah reading on the High Holidays, I asked, one of the major honors of Rosh Hashanah and Yom Kippur?

"New rabbi, they don't even ask anymore," he said, nodding up to the bimah. And then he quoted softly in Hebrew from Exodus, the eighth line of the second volume of the five books of Moses: *"Va-ya-*

kam Melech Chadash ahl Meetz'raim asher lo yada Yosafe." (There came a new pharaoh who knew not Joseph.)

I was called to open the ark holding the Torahs, and after I was done I stood next to Todd Werner, a friend from Zionist summer camp. In the old days, he loved the attention of being good-naturedly hazed and teased for his then homunculus adolescent looks. When you called him by his nickname of "Rhino Boy," he'd put his fingers atop his head like he was a creature on Marlon Perkins's *Wild Kingdom* and charge.

Now, shifting the heavy Torah to his other shoulder so he could talk to me, he pleasantly whispered, making fun of himself, that he was now head of the shul's ritual committee, which I knew from the old days to be about the only group with a voice in the running of the place that had to do with Judaism and not synagogue politics.

Todd could sing like a cantor and explain like a rabbi that week's Torah portion. Yes, he was kind of a geek, but he had the courage of his own geekdom; forever the Hebrew school goody-goody, he had always laughed at his role and allowed others to laugh too, endearing him to the wise guys. Or maybe back then, we self-styled prisoners of Talmud Torah sensed that Todd's reverence was too real and good-natured not to admire. *There was a real Jew,* I'd thought.

And he'd kept it up, I had already deduced from his permanent station on the bimah where he choreographed the smooth running of the prayers, reading from the texts, and opening and closing the ark. And I liked his kindness, as he covered up for the congregants, leading them through the correct religious paces like a gentle Arthur Murray dance school teacher.

It was reassuring that he'd grown up to be head of the ritual committee. As a Jew, he was still the real deal, and I was surprised that his kind actually existed in this suburban shul—and that I cared anymore that there was a Jew I respected for combining both knowledge and niceness.

Todd whispered to me that he was a chemist and had three kids; his wife was a woman we knew from Hebrew school. He hadn't grown an inch and seemed exactly the same, and then, out of sheer force of ancient habit, I whispered into his ear, "Hey, Rhino Boy, your underwear is falling *up*," and reached behind and grabbed the back of his belt as if to give him a wedgie, just like everybody did to him dozens of times in eighth grade in Hebrew school and at Herzl camp.

He laughed heartily, though he tried to stifle himself. He was still head of the shul's ritual committee, after all, and he needed to perform with the dignity of his office.

"You never change," he said, trying and failing to stop burbles of laughter from coming out.

"Oh, yes I do," I responded.

"Can you still read Torah?" he asked, trying to settle himself by recalling the days when we were both in heavy rotation at the old synagogue's Torah-chanting round-robin.

"Oh, *yeah*," I said sarcastically, winking. "The words go from left to right, right?"

"You ought to try again, you were good," he said.

"Thanks," I said, genuinely amazed at his insane suggestion to read Torah once more.

Unfortunately, Rabbi Matzoh (her real name) had seen us goofing around, from the faux wedgie on. And in a typical act of proper Conservative rabbi bimah outrage that I'd been inciting my whole life, she now offered a muted yell of "Sha!" and her eyebrows flared like Groucho Marx. Then, realizing she was yelling at two grown men, one an unknown putz but the other the head of the ritual committee, she immediately looked stricken.

"Sorry . . . uh, sorry," the rabbi whispered toward us, making sure Todd could hear.

"Well, Rhino Boy," I said, "you've gotten us in trouble with a rabbi on the bimah again."

I walked down from the stage and looked about at the fashions, the architecture, the expense of praying here. I was reminded me of what Dingleman, a character in Mordecai Richler's *The Apprenticeship of Duddy Kravitz,* said about a particular temple of the nouveau riche Jews of Montreal: "The few times I stepped inside there, I felt like a Jesuit in a whorehouse."

I am a better Jew than these, I grandiosely thought.

My attempts to become anything but what I was—a just plain Jew— took on ever more desperate dimensions. No longer satisfied with private displays of disaffection, I now turned my professional life into an exercise in more elaborate disguises. I became increasingly obsessed with participatory journalism.

In 1997, at almost thirty-eight, I crossed the line. For *Details* I would train as a boxer with a real coach and eventually spar with the women's world champion. My shtick before the "match" would be to sew a Star of David on my boxing trunks, just like Benny Leonard, Barney Ross, and Kid Kaplan, champions who'd punched their way out of the ghetto in the 1920s and '30s.

Then, one day at the end of my training, I broke my leg in five places. When I woke up from surgery, an infection, osteomyelitis, had wormed its way from my leg tissue and was quickly spreading through the core of my twisted limb. Recovery would take a full year, half of that on my back, and I would still probably end up walking for the rest of my life like Dustin Hoffman as Ratso Rizzo in *Midnight Cowboy.*

As the weeks on my back turned into months, the world went flat and black. Staring out my bedroom window, day after day after day, I was haunted by the time with which I could do nothing but think and bide my utter aloneness. When visitors went home, there was no more audience for my shtick.

That haunting didn't devolve into self-pity, I think. I didn't even whine about the notion of never walking normally again. Rather, it was three words on continuous loop uttered five years before: "Jew him down. Jew him down." The phrase uttered twice by my ex-wife's grandfather to my dad in the ten minutes after we were married.

It was the last time I'd been in love, the result of taking the wrong path down a road that had divided in two. I had brushed aside the slurs at the time of my wedding.

Not long after, when my marriage crashed, I talked about it only as a horrific joke, goofy, inconsequential. It had become a story, literally, published with a byline, with just three words, said twice, left out because it was a family newspaper.

Half a decade later, all I wanted to do was go back to that moment in time and take the other path. But even if I could, where would it lead?

Enslaved to myself and unable to work, I looked around for spiritual comfort. Judaism? Been there, done that, check please.

6

THE MENSCH OR
THE GOLEM

Home no longer felt right anymore, like the wrong skin for my body. Yet I was unable to figure out how to remake the place again, or move on. Anyway, the problem felt like part of my soul sickness—no matter where I ran, I knew, there I'd be. And I remembered the prime secret rule from when I was a high school bookie: The best bet was always an underdog playing at home.

Still, I'd been going it alone for a long time. And the only home I'd ever really known was Judaism. The very house I grew up in seemed Jewish in every pore. The only sense I'd ever had of actual community, even though I now despised that community, was the Jewish one in which I'd been raised.

Yet I couldn't stop longing for the other life I was missing because of my religion. I enjoyed getting in trouble in seemingly *American* teenager ways, even when they were cruel or destructive. Once, in high school, David Feinstein and I had taken a large rectangular board from in front of the Talmud Torah, the name of our Hebrew school, that had been been placed facing the street with a message writ large: "Save Soviet Jews." To that we added in spray paint, "Win Valuable

Prizes." We then sneaked down to one of the school buses and changed the "Talmud Torah" moniker on its side to "amud Torah."

I'd always hated those buses. It was embarrassing to have to get on them four days a week immediately after junior and senior high school. Hoping none of the cheerleaders or girls I liked was watching, I'd burst from the hallways to the side door, leaping at the last second into the Talmud Torah bus. Sometimes it had already begun moving, and at best my sprint to the door made me feel like an all-American outlaw like Clyde Barrow, riding away from a bank robbery on the running board of a car.

Still, from where I now stood, feeling no more spiritual than an inanimate desk, what else but Judaism did I really know? Months after seeing Rabbi Friedman on the plane, I'd increasingly felt how emotionally *right* it would be for me to try and begin everything again, as *some* kind of Jew.

Choosing Judaism seemed obvious. I wanted back what I had lost. Maybe because I didn't know about anything else. Maybe because I felt an emotional pull when I ordered kreplach at a delicatessen but nothing when I ordered ravioli, basically the same thing, at an Italian restaurant. I could have tried Zen or yoga, but other disciplines didn't connect me to a people, a lifestyle, a family system—even if I'd spent the previous two decades fleeing from all three.

Judaism was the only heritage I had or knew, a tradition that encompassed not just the religious aspects but also Yiddishkeit, the folk wisdom and traditions that go right to the heart of one's sense of identity, sensibility, and pride. Or maybe, as Heidegger said, "We pursue that which retreats from us."

"Be a mensch!" I heard my father say. "It doesn't matter how much commotion or attention you draw to yourself while you're still alive," he'd say, "you'll still need six people who care enough to put you in the ground, and ten willing to say kaddish over your grave."

A mensch. It has nothing to with temporal success or one's riches or standing in society. It means having *character,* doing what is right, carrying one's responsibility decorously and without complaints. You could be poor or unschooled and still be a mensch, while just being learned was no guarantee of anything.

In the community and family I grew up in, to be one was the highest compliment a man or woman could receive in Yiddish. A mensch was a stand-up guy or woman, a giving and forgiving person with a *Yiddishe hartz,* a warm Jewish heart. Now, I realized, that was what I was seeking. To be a mensch.

"Be a mensch! Be a man! Stop feeling sorry for yourself, do something for somebody else that doesn't have anything to do with your self-aggrandizement, that God would see as a mitzvah even if no one on earth sees it." My macho father said it over and over again.

As an assimilated adult, I'd decided the mitzvoth I carried out would come from my secular soul, not the Torah. In a way I always had my Judaism; I just didn't honor it or recognize that it was still inside me. So now I took a different approach to feeling like an authentically good person, even as I ridiculed in print everybody and everything, including myself. I overtipped waitresses, flirted with eighty-five-year-old widows, gave to the NAACP, worked every third Sunday at a Bowery soup kitchen making the bums laugh as I ladled out their broth, and a bought a pencil every day from the blind guy sitting in front of St. Patrick's Cathedral.

All this, I thought, was what made me Jewish. It was a soul thing, not something religious. To me, an Orthodox Jewish slumlord was goyish, while a Catholic who understood the subtle, all-important difference between mayonnaise and mustard was Jewish. Capital punishment was goyish, but appearing on CNN's *The Capital Gang* with Morton Kondracke was Jewish.

Still, when I did bother to think about it, I wasn't very impressed by the promotion the nameplate symbolized, to a windowed office in a midtown office building, as I cheerfully climbed the corporate hierarchy. Then, I'd hum the Joni Mitchell song under my breath, "You could have been more / than a name on the door."

Even now, I kept the defunct office nameplate on my bathroom wall as an ironic reminder of past existential escapes alongside the long-ago-framed *Magen David Zahav*, the "Golden Mogen David" award I received from my synagogue my senior year in high school "for proficiency in Torah reading and outstanding contribution to Adath Jeshurun Congregation and our community," duly signed by two rabbis, a cantor, and the shul's president.

The ache for breaking my father's heart four years later had never dissipated 100 percent. The feeling that I owed something always lingered. Still, the only thing I could think of for which I needed to repent was not just playing the absent Fifth Son at the Seder, but reveling in it.

Now, at forty, the Hebrew word *t'shuva* popped into my head for the second time since my plane trip with Rabbi Friedman. *T'shuva* means repenting by turning toward God. According to religious Jews, even if you didn't get all the way there, turning toward repentance for your sins was more than just a start for mere mortals.

Though I didn't believe in God, I did indeed have faith that hell existed on earth, and not just in lame jokes I told about my ex-wife. Even for those blessed with enough to eat every night and a roof over their heads, there was the hell they could construct out of their own lives. There was nothing incisive in knowing that.

Each hell, I thought, would be individually tailored to the person. Mine, I believed, was that I would turn into my own particular golem, the monster described in the Jewish mystical texts known as the Kabbalah, a creature with a body but no soul or feeling. Tales of the golem usually involved the monster destroying its maker. Mary Shelley modeled Frankenstein's monster after the robot from the Middle Ages.

The golem's metaphysical cousin in the Kabbalah was the much less frightening dybbuk, who in exact opposition to the monster was a soul without a body. Among other places, dybbuks were recounted in holy texts, Isaac Singer stories, Yiddish plays, and Abbie Hoffman's incorrect assertion as to why his shticking nonstop for his causes wouldn't lead him to die early or defeated: "I wouldn't say it's acting, I don't think I'm a very good actor. But there's a dybbuk inside me, greased with chicken soup, that says, 'Survive! Survive!' " Dybbuks were mischievous, not murderous like their golem cousins.

The Kabbalah was a book of hocus-pocus, I'd been taught, for crazy people, Hasids. Misunderstood, its putative Houdini-like secrets could supposedly drive people insane, or delude others into thinking they were the Messiah. It had happened. According to Talmudic law, one had to be a forty-year-old married man even to open the Kabbalah's covers.

Except for the golem and what he stood for, I wasn't interested. I had first read of the vengeful monster in my Hebrew school library while serving out my lengthy detention for the spray-paint vandalism. When the librarian disappeared for a moment, I'd pried a green volume from 1939 titled *Jewish Magic and Superstition* by Joshua Trachtenberg off a top shelf. I read of the mystical, destructive force of the golem as if it were a fairy tale. I learned how he became animated from the dust for his role as the soulless, living dead who must do his job as a protector of the Jews, then had to be immediately reduced by his maker back into ashes. Or else.

I read on. Brilliant mystics, it seemed, who knew a seventy-two-letter code name for God and some other incantations could supposedly bring a golem from the dust, but the monster was only a temporary means for fighting anti-Semitic communities and helping Jews.

When incarnated, the word *emet*—"truth"—would automatically be etched on the golem. When his good work was done, the mystic need only erase the first Hebrew letter off the monster's forehead. Now stood the word *met*—"death"—which when exposed would reduce the golem back to harmless dust.

But the mystical masters often seemed not to know when enough was enough with their golems and to have enough sense to destroy the magical thing they created. One famous story involved a medieval rabbi in Prague who allowed his golem to grow so big that he could no longer reach its forehead to turn him into dust by erasing the first letter etched there. Thinking quickly, the rabbi asked the golem to bend down and tie his shoe. When he did, the rabbi scratched away the letter—and the gigantic golem immediately turned to dust, burying and suffocating the rabbi.

The golem, I always remembered, was the monster who, if his creator went awry, would kill, unable to tell the difference between the Jew who created and idolized him and the evil outsiders he was supposed to do away with.

Now, even if I no longer believed in God a generation later, I decided I had indeed created my own personal hell, and I personified it in the form of an individualized golem I'd fashioned out of my passions and fears. My golem was a two-headed ogre, though I loved one of the incarnations that came attached to the monster I'd created.

I, too, had lost track of how big my golem—my own version of truth—had gotten. Now I could no longer reach high enough to change the letter to kill what I'd conceived, and I knew I would be suffocated like the old rabbi in the story.

The first of two parts bore the *Yiddishe kopf* of the late Abbie Hoffman, a Groucho Marxist but also equipped with a deeper meaning to and courage of his buffoonery. Knowing his ultimate, self-inflicted fate only made me quiver in fear over the symbol Abbie had been to me from a young child onward.

I knew him a little at his worst, and so did he. "I'm not the hustler I pretend to be," he said. "I've lost my share. There was just too much that couldn't be won by hustling."

Abbie and his Republican father never reconciled while my father and I had never been at war. "He could have been somebody, a doctor or lawyer," his father said. "Now we have to read the papers to see what jail he's in."

A few years later, Abbie had gone to his father's funeral, and his last surviving uncle yelled in front of the casket that Abbie's shenanigans had killed his old man.

After retelling the story, Abbie uncharacteristically shut up. Then he said, pointing at his suit coat, "I need a new one someday."

"You okay?" I asked.

He turned to me with a deep frown. All day long I'd only seen him beaming. "All these people are into is nostalgia," he said. "It's just another word for depression."

"But look at all you did!" I said, a twenty-four-year-old dope who understood nothing of dashed hopes—yet.

"Ach, a few million of us jumped up and down, and moved the world an inch."

Looking down the twenty-plus stories from where we stood, I asked him to sign a copy of his new book and an article inside called "I Remember Papa," in which he said, "I realize how much my father taught me and how much I miss him now. I know he tried his best, and I understand it wasn't his fault. . . . He passed away a loyal citizen, but with a lingering doubt that his *meshuggener* [crazy] son had some good points after all."

Six years later, the Jewish clown with a point, like I'd always wanted to be, killed himself. He hadn't gone for the gelt, he indeed had gone for broke, and despite all the millions who loved him, he died broken, despondent, and alone. Hoffman died thinking he'd killed his beloved father, a proud Jew who'd had the largest funeral Temple Emanuel in Worcester, Massachusetts, ever had—a father who never forgave the son for breaking his heart.

So the shtick that defined Abbie ultimately backfired, but I was starting to think that maybe there was time for me to kill that one head of the golem he symbolized, the clown who died with no more jokes, the attention monger who felt he had no one to say good-bye to.

The specter and icon of Abbie the rabble-rousing clown was the good head on the individualized golem I knew was the real one who would destroy me. The bad head, the grandiose father, was Joe Gould.

Over the course of the last several years, my greatest fear was that I would evolve in spirit into the infamous and wretched Joe, immortalized in the brilliant *New Yorker* writer Joseph Mitchell's series of stories titled *Joe Gould's Secret* (1966).

Midcentury, Gould was Greenwich Village's biggest pretender, con man, literary poseur, and phony street-corner philosopher, and he told Mitchell, for whom he detailed, as Gould detailed for everyone, how he was writing a book he called "An Oral History of Our Time." At that moment, he told Mitchell, the oral history was already eleven times longer than the Bible.

Gould indeed was often writing madly; he carried his notebooks everywhere, dropping them off and picking them up at odd intervals from bohemian friends. He lived off the borrowings and stealings he could glean from those who wanted to finance his alcoholic Bowery street life or putative writing project.

Finally, Mitchell stumbled upon several books and discovered that almost all of the chapters were identical. Each was an obsessive retelling of the death of Gould's father, a doctor who wanted Joe to go into the family business when he got out of Harvard and never forgave the son for instead going to New York.

There was no "Oral History of Our Time."

Mitchell didn't expose Gould until he was dead, allowing the shyster to keep what the writer called his "rice bowl," his way of, and reason for, living. Even after he died, Mitchell eulogized the faker as a "lost soul."

In a preface to a new edition of *Joe Gould's Secret* published when the movie came out, *New Yorker* writer William Maxwell put it differently. "Gould," he wrote, "went from bar to bar cadging money and drinks off friends and strangers. He must have been known to hundreds of people, few of whom would have been charitable enough to describe him as a lost soul."

Now I saw myself just as Mitchell saw Joe, a "lost soul."

I felt about my Jewishness the way Joe Gould felt about home. "In my home town I never felt at home. I stuck out. Even in my own home, I never felt at home. . . . Down among the cranks and the misfits and the one-lungers and the has-beens and the might've-beens and the would-bes and the never-wills and the God-knows-whats," he'd said, "I have always felt at home."

How Joe Gould lived scared me as much as the way he died and turned him into the second symbol topping my personal golem. An Ivy League boy from the "right" kind of family, he'd impersonated a wise man wearing fool's rags, alienated his blood, and fled forever from his father.

"I have a delusion of grandeur," Joe Gould said. "I believe I'm Joe Gould."

Luckily for me, one day, impersonating myself didn't work anymore. I realized that I would either perform my own brand of *t'shuvah* and turn toward being a mensch, or I would live and die like Joe Gould and Abbie Hoffman. "What's the matter with you, Joe? You don't seem to be yourself," one of Gould's pals told him after Mitchell, but no one else, had discovered he was a fraud.

"I'm *not* myself," Joe shot back. "I've never been myself."

Neither was I. And I had to find that person, that self, the real one. When Joseph Mitchell described Gould's oral history as a "repository of jabber, an omnium-gatherum of bushwa, gab, palaver, hogwash, flapdoodle, and malarkey," he might as well have been describing me.

My golem would do what runaway golems do—kill their creator, me. And it was almost as irrevocable a sentence as those written in the supposed Books of Life and Death on Yom Kippur.

Help.

7

TUGS

The bearer of this letter has lived a life of falsehood; he sought saintliness but removed himself from it; there is no saintly spark in him to be found.

—Rebbe Aaron of Karlin

I got out of my car and walked, with suddenly leaden feet, up to the white ranch house where Rabbi Friedman lived. It looked like the kind of all-American dwelling where June and Ward Cleaver would feel at home. I shivered, partly from a bitter Minnesota fall wind that was slicing through the inappropriately light baseball jacket that I suddenly realized I was wearing.

I stood there thinking of Abbie and Joe and their sad, pathetic fates. Now, standing in front of the door, I suddenly hoped nobody was home, that Hasidic scholar Rabbi Manis Friedman had forgotten our appointment, or that one of us had written down the wrong date. I didn't take my gloves off, or kiss my fingers and then touch the mezuzah on the doorframe, as I'd been taught.

Stamping my feet for circulation, I thought that though I barely knew him, I'd always remembered Rabbi Manis Friedman, even before our shared plane ride. And in a life once filled with rabbis of every persuasion, Friedman was one of the few I'd met whom I hadn't thought was full of shit.

A few weeks earlier, unable to get our talk on the plane out of my mind, I'd written to him after poking around a book of Jewish aphorisms in a halfhearted attempt at inspiration. Only one saying sent a shiver. The words had been uttered by the Ba'al Shem Tov, the eighteenth-century founder of Hasidism who'd been excommuni-cated by the rabbinical authorities for his troublemaking, revolution-ary ideas.

I have thought many times of our previous conversation. And I have thought about all the Jewish education I told you I'd thrown away. Besides what your first rebbe the Ba'al Shem Tov said about the "Divine spark," I've also been haunted by an old Talmudic say-ing I remembered since we talked that I learned in Hebrew school. I don't remember what rabbi said it, but he did after a man came and bragged that he'd been through the entire Torah. "You've been through the whole Torah," the rabbi said, "but has the Torah been through you?"

Even when studying all those years, I now think it all went right through me. Perhaps I need to try to study again.

For effect (I thought) I repeated to him the line from the Ba'al Shem Tov that had struck me, that "there is a spark of the Divine in every living thing, even a blade of grass." Though I had no interest in becoming a Hasid, I continued, would he be willing to discuss this? I made no mention that not only did I no longer feel the spark of the Divine within me, I no longer even believed in God—or myself. And I somehow knew I had to rediscover both to believe in either.

Now, like a grave digger with amnesia, I decided I needed to re-member the meaning of turning toward, *t'shuva,* trying to be a mensch with a *Yiddishe hartz.* And my first and only choice as a guide, if he'd take me on, wasn't serendipitous. It had to be a scholar who I hoped could teach me what I needed to know to heal—or to feel. Though I thought I was looking for a teacher, I was really looking for a guide, a

Lewis and Clark of the soul, who could help me cut through the thicket of my own desperation.

So behind that door, I thought, maybe, just maybe, was the sleuth who could give me a clue as to where to find my misplaced *Yiddishe hartz*. As I pushed the buzzer, I thought about how numb I was these days. Kisses from women I liked felt no different from punches I got in the mouth at the boxing gym. Every smile and laugh was a sham, there seemed no difference between Mozart and Mantovani, I couldn't bear to listen to any music, and even reading, my lifelong escape, was torture.

Classic symptoms of clinical depression? Not according to the esteemed psychopharmocologist I'd visited, who'd prescribed something to everyone I knew who'd had a consultation. "I could give you a prescription for Prozac right now," he said, "but it wouldn't do any good. What you have to do is deal with your life."

Cain's crime had been killing off his own blood, Abel. And now, at forty, I remembered the Abel that used to be me, who read the Torah and the four questions at the Passover Seder table and argued ancient texts with rabbis who seemed almost as old as the books themselves. If I screwed up my chanting of that week's reading, blew the pronunciation of even one vowel, I was screwing up God's words and hence the universe itself. This was no small error, we were "the People of the Book," that was the party line, and He created the universe not with thunderbolts but with these very letters of the Torah.

When I was a kid it all made sense to me, even the little old men who sat in the first few rows of the synagogue on Saturday morning following along with the Torah reading in their own holy books, which Torah readers saw as cheat sheets that provided the old men the correct vowels and notes with which the portion must be sung. Thusly armed, they waited for you to make that little mistake, so they could sadistically shout out the little correction.

But I understood what the old men were after. Without the words pronounced and chanted just so, the formula of the world itself was tampered with. Like young comics, Torah readers learned by bombing. You dealt with the hecklers by ignoring them, finding your own mistakes, or singing more loudly, straight through the shouted corrections. And eventually you had them in your hand, listening raptly, making no mistakes with God's words or notes, finishing with a dramatic flourish and walking down the steps of the stage to a swarm of handshakes, backslaps, and *yasher koach*s (congratulations for holy work well done) from the synagogue's peanut gallery.

Then, sitting down with the congregation on those long-ago Sabbaths, racing through the prayers I'd memorized years before, I'd close my eyes as tightly as I could, my prayer book pressed against my leg. And I would truly *pray,* for everything the siddur (prayer book) said to pray for. Thank you, God, for letting me wake up, and letting me go to sleep, to wake up again to thank you one more time for letting me be the kind of Jew I wanted to be, a Torah-reading, siddur-clutching, kosher-keeping Jew.

I'd come over the years to lie when asked why I'd killed off my own blood, the best part of myself, my long-ago *Jewish* self. I'd remake Cain's "Am I my brother's keeper?" into Groucho Marx's "I wouldn't belong to any club that would have me as a member," as a perfect, if unconscious, description of my own Jewish self-loathing.

At forty, I'd spent the last half of my existence running, the last several years wondering why and from whom. I'd finally come to know I had to start over—as a Jew I'd come to realize over the last several, soulless, frightening years that I wanted, *needed* to join the one club, I hoped, that would still have me as a member.

But I needed to do it *my* way this time, because otherwise I'd end up back in the darkness. If I still believed in God, it was the blackness of the kind that existed before light was separated from shadows in the first paragraph of the Bible.

For decades I'd known I didn't want to be that kind of Jew again, a prisoner of the pilpul, those endless and torturous arguments of microscopic scholarship over the meaning of every single letter in the Torah. I was left with a bagful of idioms but nothing real to say.

What had happened to drive me so far away, I wondered, and why was the spiritual drifting of the last few years turned into panicked desperation? I kept rereading F. Scott Fitzgerald's tale of his own crack-up, his soulful meditation on the horror of losing your own heart and mind.

The line about the "sort of blow that comes from within—that you don't feel until it's too late to do anything about it, until you realize with finality that in some regard you will never be as good a man again" stuck the most.

Finally I pushed the buzzer hard and faintly heard a man ask in Yiddish, *"Du herst aymetzer beim tier?"* (Do you hear someone at the door?)

Peeking through a glass panel, I saw a boy of about ten, a skullcap on his head and tzitzit (religious tassels) flying from his waist, take a running start ten yards away.

"How ya doing?" I asked when he opened up, his impish, freckled grin turning quizzical when he saw I was most definitely a stranger.

"Baruch HaShem," he said softly in response, turning his eyes away, offering the standard Hasidic reply of "fine," literally "Praise be the Name." "The name"—*HaShem*—was God, who was left out of the phrase because His name itself was not to be uttered outside of prayer.

"Ta'teh!" (Father!) the boy yelled in the direction of the study. Then he reversed his course, gliding back to a spot in the modest living room where he was boisterously entertaining his older sister by doing handstands, yarmulke held in place with bobby pins.

I was stunned—minus the tzitzit, the kid looked and acted exactly like me at his age. His way of correctly and modestly performing Jewish rituals (*"Baruch HaShem"*) then bouncing off the walls with kiddie *shpilkes* (ants in the pants) seemed to me a Hasidic version of myself from some long-forgotten memory album.

Rabbi Friedman then walked out of his library and shook my hand. I asked him how he was.

"*Baruch HaShem,*" he said.

"What do you Hasidim say if you're not doing fine?" I asked.

"*Baruch HaShem,*" he said, laughing, "and then, 'not so good.' " Even then, though, because God was everywhere and in everything, he said, you're doing fine, or at least doing the way you should be.

He then introduced me to the last two of his fourteen children still living at home, all from his wife, Chana, who was in New Jersey today visiting relatives. "We're on our own tonight," he said. "That means we can goof around."

He turned to his twelve-year-old daughter, Muschka, and then pointed to the boy who'd opened the door and said, "This is Nissan."

I nodded, still dumbstruck, looking at the little boy as if he were the Ghost of Christmas Past. We had the same name.

"Well, come in out of the cold, Nissan," Rabbi Friedman said.

I went into his study and sat down in the single industrial-looking gray metal chair to the side of his desk. Rabbi Friedman's worktable was of a similar hue and austerity, as if it had been bought from a used-office furniture store that in turn had gotten it from a high school principal's office, circa 1971. To the immediate left of the desk sat a fax machine that beeped in newspaper clips, typewritten pages, and scrawled notes, written in English and Hebrew.

Outside the office's windowed double doors, the living room seemed a veritable Hall of Fame of the entire Hasidic movement, except that the festive pictures of beaming Lubavitch that lined the walls were mostly members of Rabbi Friedman's immediate or extended *mishpocha*. One nonfamily picture was a framed, surreal photo showing more than a hundred identical-looking men in black and beards of various lengths and hues outside the Lubavitch organization's headquarters in Brooklyn for a special conclave.

A half-played chess game sat on the Friedmans' living room couch along with some children's books written in Hebrew; with one exception, there were no paintings, to uphold the commandment of having no graven images. The only art I could see was an oil coloring of the five rebbes in Lubavitch history, stretching back to the eighteenth century, walking together through a garden.

Inside the rabbi's study, the three walls were filled floor to ceiling with religious books or books on religion, some bound in ancient leather, others modern hardcovers or bent, well-read paperbacks. Space, however, had been made for a few pictures, and I took in an etching on the far wall of the late Rebbe Menachem Mendel Schneerson. I wondered again about the circumstances surrounding his curious death—had he really said he was the Messiah?

Meantime, the Lubavitchers' unpopularity among Jews was actually a reason I felt *comfortable* among them. There was little pretense to the underdog and none to Rabbi Friedman.

They were the Jews who lived poorly, in one of the gnarliest sections of Brooklyn. They sent their children to yeshivas to become Judaic study nerds, instead of to Ivy League colleges to become professionals and rich. Identified from the other side of the religious spectrum, they, like me, were considered a *shanda fur di goyim.*

Their apparent fanaticism didn't bother me; as a reporter I used to love diving into the unknown depths of fanatical subcultures to see what made them tick. No way, I knew, was I taking the Lubavitchs' form of belief to heart and back to my empty home. I'd never joined anything that I could remember.

Indeed, in search of answers so vast that I didn't really know my question, the last wise man or woman I wanted was some polished, assimilated graduate of Hebrew Union College, with tasseled loafers, a Jeep, and a good golf game, giving me his reasoned opinion based perhaps on an op-ed piece he read in today's *New York Times.*

Rather, in finding out the *emes,* the truth, *my* truth, I knew I needed to go to the edge, with someone perhaps bearing a beard to his chest and fourteen children, who could peer over a Torah text he'd memorized and come up with seventy-two different interpretations of meaning in a single word. How *can* you judge when you know the seventy-two different meanings?

Mostly, though, I trusted at least Rabbi Friedman's learnedness, even if I knew I could never opt for his lifestyle. I liked that the Hasidim were, for better or worse, who they were, made no apologies, and seemed to feel no shame about their Jewishness, unlike so many other Jews I knew.

Since scholarship had always tied me closer than anything else to Judaism, I felt I needed whatever Friedman—not just the only rabbi I liked but the only scholar I respected—had to offer as a person, friend, and safe haven from the world. "And sometimes you have to go the farthest extremes for change to happen," admitted even the anti-Hasidic intellectual in *The Chosen,* giving the men in black their due. He would be my guide toward *t'shuva.*

I wasn't looking for a replacement father to make me Jewish; I knew my father's brand of suburban, observant, judgmental Judaism, and had felt disconnected from it for years. Granted, I'd grown more judgmental about Jews than he. With Rabbi Friedman on the outer limits, I wanted the real deal to show me different possibilities, neither of which, I already knew, meant becoming a Jew like *either* of them.

After glancing at the picture of the rebbe on the wall of Friedman's study, I turned my attention back to the rabbi. Smiling for no apparent reason, he rhythmically stroked the gray beard flowing midway down his chest. He looked like a vision: half the Judaic scholar he was; half a friendly medieval Merlin.

"You seem very worried," Rabbi Friedman said.

"Ever since I moved back to Minnesota from New York ten years ago, my friends have told me I'm the most worried person they've ever seen," I said.

"I think they're right."

I felt oddly honored. At least I was best at *something*.

"So what are you so worried about?" he asked.

"I want to find a way back. I want to come in from the cold, not even necessarily to Judaism but to life. I want to come out of the dark. I don't like myself anymore. I can't write. I can't make a living anymore. I'm offensive to other Jews. I want to be a mensch."

"Live life with joy," he said simply, "like when you were ten, when I met you and saw you singing and banging the table louder than anyone else during our dinner *nigguns* [joyous, wordless melodies]. There was even joy in the way you made trouble, keeping everyone up with horseplay after lights-out. So you should live life with joy like that again, but with the heart of a mensch, guided by the Torah."

"Easier said than done," I offered weakly. I couldn't believe he remembered all those incidents. "I do want to be a mensch," I said, "at least perform *t'shuva* and turn toward—"

"You want to repent? For what?" Rabbi Friedman asked, taking the actual usage of *t'shuva*.

"Look," he said, lightening the gloom I'd brought into the room. "Laugh. Dance. Make fun of yourself. Make fun of God if you want—in the right way. Don't be too reverent about life. We have enough of that, everybody saying they have all the answers. If you want to make fun of rabbis, do that too, me included. I do."

I laughed, hard, for the first time in I couldn't remember when. This guy could make me laugh, really *laugh* from the gut. That kind of laughter had once been my greatest joy, and then it disappeared. To me, it was a miracle. I had further confirmation of my earlier small revelation. Whatever happened—even if my appeal had run out and my golem destroyed me—I'd come to the right place.

"I liked your letter," he finally said, "but I wasn't sure what you wanted."

I remembered what Bill Murray said as the modern-day Ebenezer Scrooge in *Scrooged,* after he'd been visited by the Ghost of Christmas Yet to Come and emerged not only alive but reborn. "The Jews taught me this great word," Murray said. "Schmuck. I used to be a schmuck. But the great thing is, I'm not a schmuck anymore!" But I couldn't phrase it like that to the rabbi.

Instead, I pulled out a piece of paper and read aloud from Martin Buber, the Jewish philosopher whose book *Tales of the Hasidim* had been a standard bar mitzvah present for decades. "My soul is not by the side of my people," he'd written in despair at around my age. "I want to go on living. I want my future—a new total life, for my own self, for my people within me, for myself within my people."

Silence.

"You don't like Buber?" I asked.

Friedman shrugged. "He had his agenda. He definitely had his shtick."

Rabbi Friedman then asked about my family. On my mother's side, I told him, they could trace the learned blood to my forebear Abraham Joshua Levinson, who lived in the same shtetl at the same time as Rabbi Abraham Joshua Heschel, who was arguably the most influential American Jewish theologian of the century.

And, he wanted to know, did my grandfather really come from the Russian town of Karlin?

"Yes," I said.

I'd never heard my grandfather, who spoke only Yiddish, kvetch once about anything, even the Holocaust to which he'd lost his family. When he'd died half a century later his most precious possessions besides his family were his tefillin and old-country wine press for making shtetl wine.

Still, I couldn't resist making a joke, ripping off comic Richard Lewis. "When my grandfather died," went the line, "he donated his grief to science."

In fact, my grandfather Aaron Karlen's father had been one Rabbi

Zussman, about whom I had no information. I'd found in an old Jewish encyclopedia a lengthy entry by the Rebbe Aaron of Karlin for a Hasidic dynasty that arose in the Lithuanian shtetl of Karlin in the eighteenth century. Though my grandfather shared the name and hometown of the great rebbe, I did know one thing passed down from the old country: My family had always hated Hasids.

"Is the spirit of what you're saying about your *zayda* [grandfather] true?" Rabbi Friedman asked innocently about the joke I'd made.

"Uh, no," I said. I then told him the story of my grandfather's wine press that he'd schlepped from the old to the new country to remind him of home, where his talents as a vintner made him the official maker of the shtetl's sacramental wine, bringing the family *yichus*.

"Like I told you on the plane," he said, "there's a difference between being a buffoon at your own or your family's expense and telling a joke out of joy. Like I also said, almost every comedian I've met is miserable. Is that why you wrote me? To get my permission to be a buffoon and hide behind your Jewish self? You have my permission."

His house and cell phone had rung every couple of minutes since I'd arrived, and yet he made no moves to answer them. But I sensed my time was running out here. Squirming, I had to set things straight fast. For decades, I explained, ever since I'd run away from my faith, I'd concocted, I thought, a secular place where the important thing in life was to be an ecumenical mensch.

For the warm and humane heart that came with it, I re-explained my old what-makes-a-mensch checklist wherein God was irrelevant. I thought Lutherans who left big tips for beaten-down waitresses were more Jewish than Orthodox Jews who repeated their prayers thrice daily by rote but *hondled* (bargained) with the non-Lubavitch over every price to the point that they seemed to reincarnate Shylock.

You break up with girlfriends in person and flirt with elderly ladies. You open the door for others, and hold the elevator for strangers. You keep secrets, root for your friends, and don't stab people

in the back, but call them weasels to their faces. This was a secular
mensch, and the list was infinite.

Beyond that, the only Jewish precept I believed in, I told Friedman,
was Rabbi Hillel's famous first-century dictum, "What is hateful to
you, don't do to another. The rest is commentary. Now go and study."

That's why I was here. "I want to study," I said. "I already try not to
do what is hateful to me, but that isn't working." Would he have me as
I tried my brand of *t'shuva,* turning toward trying to be a mensch?

"So you want to become a mensch and refind your *Yiddishe hartz*
by studying the Kabbalah," he asked, unimpressed, like Sergeant Joe
Friday just getting the facts.

"Yes," I said, completely disingenuous about the Kabbalah part. I
had no use for the spirituality du jour. I wanted to study with him because I trusted him.

"I really can't help you," he said gently. "Forget the Kabbalah, forget the Torah, go straight to God."

Now *he* changed the subject. "You say you're lost. Where should
you be?"

I recalled the family at that table I never said good-bye to, the un-
cles called by their Yiddish nicknames like Uncle Moish, and the aunts
with their lipstick-smeared Tareytons demanding in husky tones,
"Come here and give me a kiss, doll. You married?"

"I'm sixteen, Aunt Ida," I'd say.

"Your grandparents were engaged at five!" she'd remind me.

They were all gone, dead, lost, or forgotten. I never visited the ones
I knew to still be alive in nursing homes. They were as much a part of
my seemingly forever-lost Judaism as my ability to chant from the
Torah or sing prayers by heart.

The rituals had dwindled away from me and I'd barely been aware
of the loss; so had the people I'd actively fled from whom I'd wanted
no part of, and now they haunted me, often from the grave. "I'm no
longer a Jew," I said.

"Let's go back to the fifth son at the Seder table we talked about on the plane," he said, "the son who doesn't show up and no one talks about because they think he isn't Jewish anymore. In fact, he usually has higher expectations than anybody there."

"So again, you're saying I'm the fifth son at the table, the missing one?" I asked.

He shrugged. "I still don't know. Maybe the important thing is what you think."

He paused. "If you'd like, come back in a few days."

He paused again. "You have tefillin? Bring them in."

I instinctively flinched, remembering the embarrassment they signaled to me when I was fourteen at Zionist camp.

"Uh, yeah," I said. "I've got the ones I used at camp that my grandfather gave me for my bar mitzvah—they're pretty banged up. And I think my grandfather's own tefillin are laying around the house somewhere. I'll have to ask my father."

The front door opened, and in walked Friedman's thirty-one-year-old son Moitel, also a rabbi, who ran a local yeshiva and lived a few blocks away. "So you're a bachelor tonight?" he asked his father. "You making dinner?"

"Hot dogs," he said. "Don't tell your mother." He then looked at me and said, "Hot dogs?"

While the five of us ate, the two older Friedmans would periodically start singing *nigguns,* which they started in the midst of conversations for no reason, pounding the table with their fist for a beat, then just as quickly resuming conversation. I did not join in. I felt as out of place as a first year anthropology student the first time he visited the Masai.

The table talk circled the world of current events. ("Did you see the cartoon in the *New York Post* of an Arab child talking about his suicide bomber father, with the caption, 'Someday I want to blow up just like Daddy'?") They talked about everybody's day at work, laughed over what an idiot some guy named Yussel in Brooklyn was when he contracted for another fellow named Velvl down the block to do his kitchen cabinets. They talked of the brilliance of Thomas L. Friedman, the *New York Times'* three-time Pulitzer Prize–winning foreign affairs columnist.

There were discussions of Yiddishkeit, from how many fringes are on a tallis, to when the front door would be fixed at Fishman's Kosher Delicatessen in St. Louis Park, the only restaurant kosher enough in the Twin Cities where the Lubavitch felt they could eat.

Smiling weakly, I thought of the scene in *Annie Hall* when Woody Allen goes to Diane Keaton's hometown in Chippewa Falls, Wisconsin, to meet her anti-Semitic, Protestant parents. *Those* people I knew how to handle.

Meantime, Rabbi Friedman would alternate from *nigguns* to jokes of various philosophic dimensions. "I live at the end of a one-way, dead-end street. How did I get there?" he'd ask.

Fidgeting like an atheist in church, I had to say *something* as everybody swapped tales. So I shticked. I told every single Henny Youngman one-liner I knew, answering no question with a straight answer.

"There's a new insurance policy for guilt-stricken Jews," I said. "It's called 'My Fault Insurance.' "

They laughed; they hadn't heard that one; they all said they'd remember it. I felt accepted, not pitied, and I went on, the warm feeling shaking my body again.

"Why did Golda Meir turn down the Suez Canal? No boardwalk!"

I kept going. "Two elderly Jewish ladies run into each other at their apartment's elevator. 'Do you see what's going on in the Middle East, China, Africa?' one asks. 'I didn't see anything,' the other says. 'I live in the back of the building.' "

In just two meetings, at his house and on the plane, I'd grown comfortable with Rabbi Friedman. His sense of humor, his ultramellow demeanor of take it easy but pay attention, it's only life, made it not only bearable but also enjoyable to be with him, shooting the breeze with this ultrafundamentalist. He listened like a good reporter, a virtually unique but fantastic trait in rabbis. But to my family, I was sleeping with the enemy. So aghast were the half of Russia's Jews who were against the Hasidim that they didn't even have to name who or what they were aghast at. These anti-Hasids were *mitnaggim,* literally, "againsters." Ever since the Hasidim had emerged, I'd been told by my family, my ancestors up through the present had been militant "againsters."

Did he have any advice, I asked Rabbi Friedman, about what to tell my friends and family who were already voicing concern that I was spending any time with a Hasid? What could I tell them when they invariably quizzed me with, "You aren't going to turn into one of *them,* are you?"

"Tell them you *are,*" he'd said before dinner, "and if you don't, you'll know the reason *why not.*"

It was as close as he ever came to proselytizing, and I never once had to feed him Groucho's line about never joining a club that would have me as a member—and as far as I could tell, the Lubavitch would take *anybody.*

8

THE HASID
EVERYONE LIKES

One runs away to find oneself, and finds no one at home.

—Joan Didion

Our second meeting at Rabbi Friedman's house began benignly enough. I was immensely pleased there even *was* a second talk; I'd requested in my letter only one audience. Rabbi Friedman showed me into his study and we exchanged pleasantries.

I was properly introduced to Mrs. Friedman as she entered, and he then left the room. I stuck out my hand to shake hers. The move was as appropriate as offering her a pork rib sandwich, and my hand stayed in the air like the floating lightbulb magic trick. I had forgotten that Hasidic women are not allowed to be touched by any men but their husbands. "Well, so much for those good initial impressions," I said to her, not believing what I'd done.

"Don't worry," she said, laughing reassuringly. "It happens all the time."

Despite her nonchalant kindness, I called *strike one* on myself via some invisible umpire standing behind me like Casey at the bat.

"What do I call you?" I asked. "Rebbetzin?" I ventured, using the Yiddish honorific used by most rabbis' wives.

She scrunched up her face, laughed again, and said please, not that.

"Mrs. Friedman?" I tried.

"Call me Chana."

"Okay, Chana."

"I'm around," she said cheerfully.

And then she wasn't.

In addition to his scholarly credentials, I knew it was just as important for me to be with Rabbi Friedman because he was funny, both one-liner funny and observational funny.

And I knew I had to laugh again, really *laugh*—like I had at that first meeting, laughing from the bottom of my gut. Losing that ability and a true sense of humor was among my greatest losses, and if I were ever going to heal I had to have that back, for good, for use on my own. I'd forgotten how, and I sensed it was a shortcut out of my despair.

"I kind of need you," I said, trying to sound somehow laconic but my voice trailing off in his study, "you're not like the others . . ."

"Yeah, I'm the token Hasid everybody likes," he said self-mockingly.

But it was true. When the Hasids wanted to take over an idle plant in rural Postville, Iowa, and turn it into a kosher slaughterhouse, Friedman was sent as the emissary to talk the local farmers into saying yes. Facing a leery, seed-hat-wearing crowd of two hundred in the town's city hall, Friedman broke the ice by trying to explain to people who'd never actually seen one what Jews were.

"If you've got two Jews," he told the farmers, saying a joke I myself had told in self-loathing at that boxing party but that he used for ex-planation, "you'll have three opinions." We were using the same mate-rial: me for self-debasement at boxing parties; he in Iowa, everybody laughed, and the kosher slaughterhouse came to Postville.

Rabbi Friedman's wife then entered the study. "Manis," she said, "you'll probably want to take this phone call."

I peered around the place from the doorway of Rabbi Friedman's study. Downstairs were numbered rooms that could be filled with dozens of visitors on holidays. Around the corner from his office was a kitchen and dining-room table that were big enough to prepare and serve a banquet, yet like furniture in a fun-house mirror, the cooking and eating space looked intimate enough for a dinner for three.

I'd always been drawn to the profane and blasphemous, even when I was a good Jew. Could even the profane, a Jew who mocked Judaism, come up with his own interpretations of the religion? Could *I* make up my own Judaism, or would it at least help me define what kind of Jew I could become again, if any? Would it give me back my *Yiddishe hartz*?

"Just because someone is profane doesn't mean he's not wise enough to have left behind a valuable commentary," Rabbi Friedman said to me a few minutes after he returned from his phone call.

"We didn't really get to talk about your letter the first time we met last week," Rabbi Friedman continued, and he looked at me silently for several moments, stroking his beard from chin to chest. "I was quite surprised to hear from you. It was a nice letter."

"Thank you. It's the only thing I've written in months."

"Really?"

"Really."

I then told him that though I didn't want to jump from a bridge, and hadn't come for therapy of any kind, for years I'd been nearing the abyss and had wanted to peer into it, spiritlessly running out the clock. "You must have talked to a lot of people over the years who *did* want to commit suicide," I said.

Rabbi Friedman nodded.

"What do you say?"

"They come and tell me, 'My life has no meaning, my family counts for nothing, I'm a terrible human being, I've accomplished not a thing,' the usual. And I say, 'Why stop there? Why not stick around and at least come up with a full list? You're also boring, unpleasant, sloppy, you're a terrible friend, your jokes aren't funny . . .' "

I couldn't help but laugh. The guy had timing, no question.

"They laugh too. That usually gives them the distance to see that the world is not revolving around them. Yet at the same time you have to impress upon them that *HaShem* needs them, even in their present form, when they feel so broken. He needs their mitzvoth, done their particular way, with all their particular faults and shortcomings. God still needs them to do right."

"Why does He need *anything* from us?" I asked.

"We are each married to Him, and it's a kind of partnership where He needs us to perform His mitzvoth as much as we need His light. But He needs us to do our mitzvoth, good deeds, in our own individual way, no matter our background, or how damaged we are, or our individual circumstances. He got a good deal in the marriage," he said, laughing.

"God needs those good deeds, done *your* way," Friedman went on. "*That's* your purpose. We were all put here whatever way we are for a reason. It's okay to be a schlemiel, if that's what you were born to be. It's not great, but if a kick in the pants won't change you, so be it. The sole blasphemy is to say 'if only'—'If only I were born like this, if only I had this kind of parents, if only I were someone else.' Even if we'd been granted our 'if onlys,' we'd still end up exactly as we are, struggling with the same problems of being good and moral in a world that still needs fixing."

"And that convinces people not to off themselves?" I asked. "And how do you fix things, like a broken *Yiddishe hartz*?"

"The Torah," he said, "is a how-to manual that shows us how to fix the world, and ourselves."

"How do we know we have any idea what God is talking about?" I pulled out a sheet of paper with some piece of Jewish arcana on it, just as I used to do to try and outwit and nonplus my Hebrew teachers. This saying came from the same book of Jewish aphorisms where I'd found the founder of Hasidism's mention of the Divine spark even in every blade of grass. "Your own Ba'al Shem Tov mentioned man's inability to interpret God's word," I said, reading. " 'Why does Torah begin with the second letter of the Hebrew alphabet, *bet,* rather than the first letter, *alef?* To show you that you do not even know the first thing about it.' "

He smiled in good humor, still looking completely witted and plussed.

"We just have to read, study, and *try* to understand the directions," he said.

As we talked, I looked again around Rabbi Friedman's office and the framed portrait of the late Rebbe Schneeerson on the back wall. Near the end of Schneerson's life, when it still wasn't clear that there would be no new rebbe, Friedman had been publicly named by a Jewish paper in California to be on the short list of likely successors.

He was also called to move to action equally judgmental audiences of Hasids across North America during the weeks surrounding the tenth anniversary of the rebbe's death. He continued to give stern but good-natured lectures to hundreds of assimilated Jewish singles across the country to stop looking for the perfect mate and just get married—even if that means to the person sitting right next to you. His secular 1990 book on relationships, *Doesn't Anyone Blush Anymore?,* was still in print and had been raved over by everyone from the head rabbi at Oxford University to the editors of *Seventeen* magazine.

He was the man, and I was a faux-balanced forty-year-old in search of Jewish self-improvement through scholarship, and I thought that was why he decided to hear me out.

"No, not really," he said.

"Then what was it?" I asked, thinking I'd covered everything I'd covered.

"Gedalia Goomberg," he said, slyly smiling. "You remembered Gedalia Goomberg."

Somehow I *had* remembered Gedalia Goomberg. The story emerged out of nowhere last Yom Kippur, from some field from the past, when I'd initially written Rabbi Friedman. It was like an Oliver Sacks case, where an adult who'd been banged on the head could suddenly remember every statistic of every baseball player in the major leagues in 1967 but wasn't aware of whether he was living in Minnesota during January or June.

I included the entire story in the letter, though I knew it was a sort of stupid thing to mention while trying to sound adult, mature, scholarly, and well reasoned: lyrics to a kiddie song from a generation ago in the middle of a missive to Rabbi Friedman. This time, it turned out, the song and my remembering it verbatim a generation later were revelations to him, and he laughed heartily, promising to try and dig up the old record for when I next came, my third visit to his home. I wasn't sure if he'd been moved or simply tickled that I'd remembered the generation-old song he used to pound out with dozens of children accompanying him.

Rabbi Friedman went to his closet, took out an old children's album bearing a picture on the cover of a friendly giant, and placed it on an equally old gray industrial-looking record player of the kind used in elementary school classrooms in the 1960s. Once again, I heard the tale of the giant Gedalia Goomberg, a figure of golemlike strength who still bore a *Yiddishe hartz,* the lyrics as fresh from thirty years before as any song in my CD collection.

Gedalia, the seventeen-foot-tall behemoth who could put up a building in minutes but dropped his load of bricks the moment evening fell on Friday. Gedalia, the astronaut who befriended Martians and converted them to Judaism, the ETs joyfully shouting, "We will / We will!"

And Gedalia himself and his oft-repeated chorus: "Ain't gonna work on Saturday / Ain't gonna work on Saturday! / Double, double, triple pay / Won't make me work on Saturday / It's Shabbos Kodesh [the holy Sabbath]."

"Read the Torah portion each week," he said in conclusion. "We'll talk about it if you want, but just read it. That and bringing in tefillin and doing it every morning but Shabbos are my only two requirements."

9

THE WORST GUEST

Nonsense is nonsense. But the history of nonsense is scholarship.
—Professor Saul Lieberman, one of the world's leading
Talmudic scholars, introducing Gershom Scholem for
a speech on mysticism at the Conservative Jewish
Theological Seminary in the early 1940s

We sat down to eat before we studied next time; it now seemed natural for me to take a place at the table at Rabbi Friedman's elbow. As we all washed our hands and said the prayers before eating, I took a quick accounting of my progress.

Just that act, I knew, meant I was still nowhere near to rounding the corner toward menschhood. Those with a pure heart don't keep score of their good deeds, or announce their righteousness, even to themselves. Yet looking back over the last weeks, I could already detect changes in human behavior, not just in my personal mind-set. As best I could, I was trying to turn toward not cutting moral corners.

To start, I engaged in pilpuls of my own, trying to dissect with Talmudic logic the morality of some of my actions. After I'd broken my leg, the state of Minnesota had given me a handicapped parking permit good through 2006. After I could walk, of course, I never once parked in a handicapped zone—even if I didn't believe in a hell, I believed one would be immediately invented for anybody who would do such a dastardly act.

However . . . the state also had a law that people with handicapped stickers didn't have to pay parking meters. Wasn't it okay, I'd thought, imagining I was some sort of rebel, to park at a regular meter and not pay? Wasn't I just ripping off the Man while not taking advantage of my permit so a handicapped person wouldn't lose a place?

No. After months of taking advantage, it took only about three seconds to realize that no matter what act of Trotskyite sedition I thought I was performing, I was actually just a thief.

I also tried to put into effect some of the things I'd learned in my studies with Rabbi Friedman. In the Torah portion *Ki' Tetze,* I'd read how farmers should leave one tenth of their crops in the field to be picked up by widows and orphans. Why not just gather it all and distribute the tenth to the poor? No answer.

Shame, I figured. No real mensch would shame a poor person by handing him charity when the potentially embarrassing scene could be avoided.

So whenever I was downtown eating and could scrape together a doggie bag, I'd leave it in the lobby of the public library or the Greyhound station, where the homeless, the junkies, and the insane hung out . No one said thank you, which was as it should have been.

And, as the chapter kept pointing out, a tenth of whatever is yours goes to the widows that way and the orphans this. And so, though I wasn't making much, I began giving away one tenth of that not much—which, when mentioned, becomes a mitzvah that doesn't count in my personal elucidation of proper Judaism.

Still, lots of Jews put their names up on walls for money they'd given and it counted as tzedakah, charity, one of the major tenets of Judaism and especially to the Lubavitch Hasidim. Walk into virtually any space or bedroom in the Friedman house, and you'll find on the dresser a blue and white metal *pushke,* a charity box where one was supposed to drop coins whenever possible. Besides my tithe, I came to put a *pushke* of my own in my apartment and tossed loose cigarette money into the coin slot when I could.

One commandment in the chapter said that if a couple gets married, and war breaks out, the man doesn't have to join the army and fight for a year. I liked the kindness of it and tried to take its let-everybody-have-some-slack-and-give-'em-a-fucking-break attitude into my own life: trying to see things from others' perspectives, not judging or gossiping. *Trying.*

I also stopped debasing myself and the tribe I'd been born into. Gone were the Holocaust jokes, the endless vaudeville hurly-burly indicative of nothing, and the made-up stories of my relatives. I no longer ran the other way when I saw a Jew from my high school.

And I kept my secular definitions. Macaroons were still Jewish, while lime Jell-O was goyish.

Ironically, it was at Rabbi Friedman's home where a *ger* (stranger) like me would be taken in and accepted for what he *wanted* to be, even if he wasn't yet and might never be. Not a Hasid, but a mensch. After only six weeks of our reacquaintance, I at long last felt as if I hadn't put myself on trial with Rabbi Friedman as judge and jury. As a sign of my own desperation, I'd had that feeling ever since I began coming and asking for his scholarly insight. And all he wanted to do, it seemed, was talk.

Still, Rabbi Friedman wasn't taking out his calendar to make future appointments for lessons for me. Instead, he went to his bookshelf and took out a half dozen books. "Here," he said, "take these home and see what you think."

He obviously, I assumed, planned on having me do a careful exegesis each week not only on the Torah portion but also on Rashi's interpretation of it. Yikes, this was going to be harder than Hebrew school.

I thanked him and put the books on the floor, including a leather-bound copy of Rashi (Rabbi Shlomo ben Isaac of medieval France) and his epic commentary on the Torah. The Rashi book, which came complete with the Torah portions from Exodus, was on the bottom of my pile. Friedman looked down wordlessly at my hideous gaffe, until I no-

ticed what I'd done. I'd known since about age three not to put any reproduction of the Torah, or the works of a scholar such as Rashi, on the
floor. Even if you kept such books on a table, you certainly didn't put
anything *atop* them. *Strike two,* I thought, remembering my faux pas
with Mrs. Friedman at the previous meeting.

"Uh, sorry," I said, sweeping up the books, as I suddenly wondered
why I'd never bothered to wear a yarmulke out of simple respect to
the rabbi's house. With that, I had violated a rule I'd followed for virtually any secular story or subculture I was trying to pierce: Don't pretend you're one of them, but show them the respect of their own
beliefs. For bands, that meant helping carry equipment. For baseball
teams, that meant not venturing past the first few rows of seats on the
team bus into the land reserved for players. For Hasidim, a simple yarmulke would have done it. *Strike three.*

You're out.

We talked for a while more. "I found this strange coincidence,
though," I said, taking out of my satchel a xeroxed page from the 1965
edition of *The Encyclopedia of the Jewish Religion*. "Look at this," I said,
bringing up Karlin again.

Karlin: Suburb of Pinsk; seat of Hasidic dynasty and center of
Lithuanian Hasidism. The dynasty was founded by Aaron of K.
(d. 1772), who was outstandingly successful in winning adherents
to his cause.

"So this guy is Rabbi Aaron of Karlin," I said. "And my grandfather's name was Aaron Karlen, from Karlin. I found out about this
rebbe and his dynasty by mistake ten years ago, while researching what
had happened to the rest of my grandfather's family during the Holocaust."

"Yes, Reb Aaron was a great one," Rabbi Friedman said. I thought
I detected a little stir of interest coming from the previously noncom-
mittal form sitting a few feet away. Russia's eighteenth-century Rebbe

Aaron of Karlin is still viewed as a holy sage by all Hasidim, rare when it comes to founders of other dynasties among the often-warring sects of the ultra-Orthodox.

So, for example, the Lubavitch have no more regard for the teachings of the eighteenth-century Rabbi Nachman of Bratslav (the venerated founder of the Bratslaver group of Hasidim) than they would for those of Billy Graham. But they have never had any problem with the holiness of Rabbi Aaron of Karlin, one of the leaders of the second generation of disciples after the Ba'al Shem Tov, the eighteenth-century founder of Hasidim.

Martin Buber and Elie Wiesel devoted pages in their collections of Hasidic wisdom to stories about the apparently big-time rebbe who shared my grandfather's name, Aaron (Aharon in Hebrew) Karlen.

"In Hasidic literature he is, to this day, referred to as the great Rebbe Aharon of Karlin," Wiesel writes in his investigations of the Hasidim, concerning this master who renounced his bourgeois nonreligious upbringing and all his worldly goods while stepping off his golden carriage and suddenly realizing the truth of the Divine.

"[Rabbi Aaron of Karlin] was a handsome man of great vitality," Wiesel notes, "endowed with an irresistible power of persuasion. . . . He traveled through towns big and small, spreading the Hasidic message, igniting sparks and setting crowds of listeners aflame. . . . Practically alone, he stormed the traditional rabbinic fortress in Lithuania, shaking its very foundations. Faithful in friendship, loyal to his teachers and disciples, fearless in his undertakings, he was the spearhead of the new movement. . . . The *Maggid* of Mezeritch [Hasidim's leader following the death of the Ba'al Shem Tov] loved him—and so do I. The *Maggid* called him 'our best offensive weapon.' "

"I have one story in particular I like about Reb Aaron of Karlin," Friedman said, indicating his further approval. "The first part of the story is that some of his Hasidic disciples who'd come to see his lectures were preparing a mikvah [ritual bath] of hot water for Reb Aaron to purify himself when he came to their town, and one of the young men spilled a bucket of scalding water on himself. Reb Aaron simply touched the young man's forehead, and he was healed."

Faith-healing hokum, I thought, the kind of abracadabra mysticism Rabbi Friedman and the most scholarly Hasidism, the Lubavitch, saw as hooey, or at least unlikely. Then again, Reb Aaron was a Hasidic master, so he would have the power to even make or disassemble a golem like the one on my back. Could it possibly be that I might somehow descend from an ancient master and not generations of peasants? The notion was a thrill, as if the original Eliza Doolittle discovered she was part of the royal family.

"Could it be?" I asked Rabbi Friedman. "Could I be related to the great rebbe?"

"Maybe," he said noncommittally. "There was no other reason to *be* in Karlin unless you were a Hasid."

Forget theology. I wanted a connection to an ancient master, to feel my blood or soul was richer than it was.

"But that's not the end of the story," he resumed. "Before Reb Aaron's next trip to the town, the first Lubavitcher rebbe, Schneur Zalman of Liadi, visited, and Reb Aaron's very loyal disciples went to hear him out of curiosity. They fell in love with him and his teachings. They didn't know what to do—you can't have two loyalties. But how could they tell Reb Aaron without offending the great man? The next time Reb Aaron came to town, the young men finally decided to send a delegation of three to tell the great master they wouldn't be coming to his lecture that night. They were terrified. But they had to be honest."

This, I wondered, showed how great the man who shared my grandfather's name and hometown was? That he'd been trumped by the founder of Friedman's own sect?

"So the three men finally summoned the courage to go to Reb Aaron and tell him that they'd fallen in love with the teachings of someone else. One of them at last said it. And Reb Aaron was quiet for a long moment. He then looked up at the delegation and said, 'It's been a long time since I've seen such fine young men.' He was so moved by their courage and honesty in coming to him, and not just hiding out and skipping his lecture, that he praised their defection."

"Nice guy," I said.

"The kicker," Rabbi Friedman said, "is that one of the three young men sent to tell him the bad news was the one whom Reb Aaron had healed on his last trip through town."

The tale Friedman told didn't matter as much as the fact that he was taught it, remembered it, and passed it on. To tell a story of someone, to quote and remember an ancestor or sage, is one of the Hasidim's highest symbols of respect. And about a rival Hasidic leader!

"Honestly, is there any way I could be related to Rebbe Aaron of Karlin?" I asked excitedly again.

"Maybe, it could be important," he said without a hint of con man, though I was ripe for conning. "You say your family was from Karlin? What were they?" he inquired, asking which of the three nonlost tribes of Israel my family came from.

"Levis."

"Really." Now he seemed definitely impressed; he sat up straighter in his chair, stopped drumming his fingers on the tabletop during extended pauses, didn't even look at the phone as it ceaselessly rang. He asked if I knew how important it was to be a Levi.

Well, I remembered *that*. Until the sixth century B.C., when the First Temple was destroyed, the Levite tribe was considered the equal of the high priests, the Cohanim. Moses was a Levi. When the priesthood was reorganized, the Levis dropped a notch in status but were still in charge of taking care of the Second Temple, from administration to performing the music inside.

It was still a big deal to be a Levi. On Yom Kippur, they were given the special honor of washing the holy feet of all the congregation's Cohanim. My grandfather was so proud of coming from the Levis that it was the one thing he insisted be put on his tombstone.

My mind, however, was on royalty, not tribes. "So you *really* think I might share blood with the great Rabbi Aaron?" I asked one more time.

"Maybe," he repeated, "maybe maybe."

"Well, then, we've got a problem, or at least a mystery," I said. "Like I told you before, my grandfather was a dedicated *mitnaggid*. He hated the Hasidim."

"Like I said, after Reb Aaron came to town, there was no reason to *be* in Karlin if you weren't a Hasid," Rabbi Friedman responded.

Now, through this sudden spectrum of possible exalted ancestors, I thought I felt a slight turning of the tables with Rabbi Friedman. It seemed that he would now feel as honored to teach me as I would to listen to what he had to say—or just to be in his company.

He went to a closet of his study and took out a small box of photographs. "Come," he said, motioning me out of his office and toward the kitchen table, "let's see if we can find you from the old days."

Chana had finished quizzing Nissan on his homework and joined us as Rabbi Friedman began thumbing through pictures from the early seventies. He put down several photos of youth groups visiting for weekends at the mansion the Hasids once rented, and though I recognized several people, I wasn't in there. "You disappeared," he said.

"That was from right around the time I visited, but I'm not in there. But I really didn't disappear until later."

Rummaging through the box, Rabbi Friedman began picking out different old pictures. Here was one taken soon after he'd been ordained at the Montreal yeshiva and sent to Minnesota, where he looked properly scruffy for the times in his short, scraggly black beard, casual clothes, and winter hat that covered his yarmulke.

In the picture, he is standing on a street corner on the University of Minnesota campus. Rabbi Friedman is debating with a broad smile on his face a Hare Krishna, who is unsuccessfully trying to force a Hare Krishna text into Friedman's hands, which are jammed into his pockets, accepting nothing. In the background is a small van into which the young rabbi would try to get young Jews, practicing or fallen, to come in and put on tefillin, the calling card of the Lubavitch.

The next picture out of the box was from a few years later, at a lectern, with Rabbi Friedman giving a plaque to a tall young man with a handlebar mustache. "That's Ken Holtzman, he wasn't a very good pitcher, I think he played for the Yankees," he said.

"Oh, he was pretty good. He pitched for the Oakland Athletics when they won those three World Series in a row right around the beginning of the 1970s. And he once threw a no-hit ball game. And I remember he wouldn't pitch on Yom Kippur."

"Really!" He sounded genuinely interested.

And then he took out another picture, and I pulled the grandest idiot move of the night. In the early 1970s, the founder of the Transcendental Meditation movement bought the campus of a defunct college in Iowa and named it Maharishi International University, after himself.

Friedman and another fellow had gone down there to debate, and now before me lay a black-and-white shot of the two young men with broad smiles in front of the large entrance sign bearing the college's name.

In the picture, young Rabbi Friedman was on the left. "Do you recognize the other guy?" he asked.

"I do!" I said, happy finally to see a face I'd once been connected with. It was one of my old Hebrew school teachers, a fiery Moroccan named Shabtai Hadjby. "That's Shabtai T'zvi!"

You couldn't have cut the silence with a guillotine. Rabbi Friedman looked at his wife, and they both looked at me. Shabtai T'zvi (1626–1676) was the false messiah who'd come closest to destroying a significant portion of the world's Jews' belief in anything at all. A brilliant scholar, he'd pored over the mystical books and come to the conclusion that he was God and would liberate Palestine from Turkish rule and return the land once again to a Jewish state. As charismatic as a rock star leading an audience to sing his own song, Shabtai T'zvi gained hundreds of thousands of followers, and he set off on a donkey from Middle Europe to Palestine.

When he got to Turkey, the sultan immediately imprisoned him and gave him the choice of instantly becoming a Muslim or suffering a just as instant death. Barely blinking, he donned a turban, took on the Islamic name Mehemet Effendi, destroying the faith of unheard of numbers of Jews who'd believed his interpretation of God's Oral Law.

Ooops.

"I mean that's Shabtai *Hadjby*," I said quietly. "Sorry."

Strike three, four, five, six, seven, eight, nine. Three outs. My side was through.

Or was it? All Friedman did after the initial shock was stroke his beard and say nothing. Finally, he asked, "Can you come next Thursday?"

He was forgiving me, I realized, the way a teacher would a novice pupil. I didn't feel patronized, though; I was *in* for a fourth lesson.

10

REVELATIONS, AND RABBIS WHO SAY, "I DON'T KNOW"

What is a true Hasid? Beneath a torn overcoat, inside a hovel, a heart broken but yearning for perfection. And that yearning in itself is enough. . . . God does demand much, sometimes even the impossible—but He leaves it up to man to choose the means by which to attain perfection.

—Elie Wiesel, explicating and paraphrasing
the teachings of Rebbe Aaron of Karlin

I arrived at my next meeting with Rabbi Friedman once again sans tefillin. It still felt, as they say in twelve-step speak, like a "boundary issue." During the previous week, before our fourth meeting, my grandfather's tefillin had taken on the significance of a just-found, mismatched fireplace poker that's discovered to be an heirloom.

It was purely narcissistic, of course, but I had no idea that successfully navigating back to and through the path not taken in my life would involve more than just aiming for self-improvement. It would mean trying to connect with my blood, stop feeling sorry for myself, and begin living in a *Jewish* way, however I ended up defining Judaism. If, that is, I even could.

"Oops, I forgot my tefillin," I said, but I could tell he saw right through me. I'd been lying to rabbis all my life, but I sensed Rabbi Friedman was the one who knew. I felt guilty; he'd already given me so much, and I'd withheld the one thing he wanted.

He held up his palms. "To be honest," he said, "the important thing is that you bring in tefillin and we get going on *you*."

The week's portion was Yitro, or Jethro. At least I had done my homework. And I began telling Rabbi Friedman that if *Reader's Digest* were to offer a condensed version of the Torah, Yitro would have to go in virtually unabridged. Here is where God gives Moses the Ten Commandments, which will operate for untold millennia as the world's moral compass. After studying for half an hour I realized it actually was a pleasure to contemplate the texts: It didn't feel like the dreaded Talmud torture homework, I did for a decade at Hebrew school.

"Stick with the Torah for now," he said.

"Okay," I went on. "What did unexpectedly pop out of the *parsha* to me was the phrase 'a stranger in a strange land.' It's where Moses names his son Gershom, after the Hebrew *ger*, you know, the word that means 'alien, refugee, sojourner'?"

"I know *ger*."

"Anyway," I continued, "I noticed the word *ger* appeared twice in the very same sentence, in case anyone missed the point. Do you know Robert Heinlein's sci-fi classic *Stranger in a Strange Land*?"

He shook his head. I plowed on.

"Well, the phrase Heinlein took from here also aptly describes the diaspora Jews over the last two thousand years, existing on the whims of host countries who would love their Jews one day and suddenly decide to burn their Jews at the stake the next."

Rabbi Friedman pressed together the matching fingers on each hand and looked straight ahead.

"Ever since Jesus," I continued, "the Wandering Jew has been cast as the archetypal stranger in a strange land, right?"

"Go on."

"Well, the Wandering Jew, the stranger, has proved a never-ending source of anti-Semitic stereotypes. You only have to see newsreel footage of refugees fruitlessly trying to escape Europe and World War II because they had nowhere to go and nowhere to return. Even Jewish rock singers, whether they mean to or not, seem to understand the horrific notion of being a Jewish stranger in a strange land. You know that song that goes, 'to be on your own / with no direction home / like a rolling stone'?"

He said nothing.

"Okay, so Moses probably wouldn't have put it that way if he had to explain why he named his son Gershom. But the big questions remain. Do Jews assimilate into nothingness, you know, like the Moabites or Hittites or the Philistines? Or do we find truth in our own land, at all costs and under all circumstances? Personally, I have no idea. But I think that if Jews think they are chosen, then the title comes with sometimes difficult obligations."

"Like what?" he asked.

"Like offering the compassion to the stranger that Jews themselves have always been denied. I mean, I looked ahead to the next *parsha*—it says, 'For you were once strangers in Egypt,' i.e., Jews should know better than to turn their backs on the *ger.*"

I put away my notes.

"So?" I asked

"Good," he said, smiling.

A warm shudder went through my spine to my head and limbs. *Good.*

That day, sitting in Rabbi Friedman's home, I didn't feel like a *ger.* I still had zero desire to be a Hasid, but within these walls I felt the safety among the Lubavitch that they felt as active participants in God's world. I suppose this is why people join cults, but the feeling of being a *ger* who is accepted as a worthy visitor, *somewhere,* no matter how different and strange he might be to his hosts, felt different, like nothing I'd experienced in decades.

The formal study of each week's portion or Rashi's commentary upon it was a rarity. Rabbi Friedman's assignments were to read both the Torah and Rashi, yet unless I had a specific question or wanted to get into the readings in depth, he didn't push or even ask. Sometimes if I had a general question that I thought was provocative—say, "Are these interpretations open to question?" or "How are women and gentiles really perceived in these writings?" or "Why was the Oral Law written down?"—he would pull out an arcane book like *Pirke Avot* (*Sayings of Our Fathers*) to try to deduce an answer.

Though our studies didn't have a cast-in-stone syllabus, it was obvious after a while that Rabbi Friedman had a plan of scholarship that was equal parts reading and simply living and hanging out. Part was being passed the gefilte fish at the table and slapped on the back to sing *nigguns;* another was hearing stories of the rebbes and Steven Wright jokes following the grace after meals.

I felt as if I were simply asked to join them and not judge, just as they didn't judge me, and every time I stopped over for my weekly lesson and dinner I did share in their revelation of real joy. If I were religious I would have called it an epiphany, but instead I experienced it as a giant lightbulb going on over my head.

Rabbi Friedman sat there silently, not looking especially interested but just letting me talk and talk. " 'My father didn't know what to make of me,' " I read Joe Gould saying. " 'It made me feel sorry for him—it wanted me to make it up to him, . . . "Father, I've decided I'd like to study medicine." '

" ' "That'll be the day,' "[Gould's] father said . . . and a look of intense sadness passed over [Joe's] face," Mitchell recounted. " ' "I held that remark against my father for a long time," [Joe] continued. "Every once in a while, through the years, I'd remember it, and it would cut me to the quick." ' "

I looked up from the book. "This," I said, "from a man who for fifty years nobody could say anything mean enough to to bother him in the least."

"Abbie Hoffman, Joe Gould, what is this with everybody wanting his son to become a doctor?" Friedman asked. "It's not like anyone was born to be a doctor. They were *born* as individuals, and later they studied and simply were qualified to *take* the job of becoming a doctor."

Back to Gould. "That's sad," he continued. "He was disconnected from his past. Did he die early?"

I felt uneasy. I could feel that we were heading inexorably toward my family, and my father, "the doc-tah," as his many elderly Jewish patients called him.

I was right. "Did you ever want to be a doctor like your father?" Friedman asked.

"Naah. I would have killed somebody every day. I'm like Joe Gould—I'm 'ambisinistrous,' left-handed in both hands."

"So what did your father want for you?" he pressed on.

"I was supposed to stay a Jew."

"And you didn't?"

"I was going to make my little revolution from within Judaism. Just as you told me you were 'the Hasid everybody likes,' I would be the equivalent outlaw Jew on the other end of the spectrum." What a putz.

"Hmmm," he said, sighing the way I'd learned was his way of expressing doubt.

I struggled on. "I'd practice Judaism my way, whatever way that turned out, as long as it involved at the end a capital-f Faith."

He listened expressionless. Trying to change the subject, I slid into shtick, a swamp I fall into when I'm nervous.

"Hey, you know the joke about when Judaism considers a fetus viable?"

Friedman tensed. The Hasidim, unlike most other branches of Judaism, had taken a never-ever-ever stance against abortion, one of the reasons they'd become allies with the Christian far right. They don't believe in turning off the ventilators that keep alive brain-dead patients. These souls, be they comatose rebbes or fetuses with genetic de-fects, belong to God, the Hasidim believe. It was a God who could perform miracles today, upon unborn children whose sonograms showed Down syndrome, or Harley-Davidson riders who hadn't been wearing a helmet when they flew over their handlebars at ninety miles per hour.

"No," he said, hesitantly, "I haven't heard that joke."

"When does Jewish law consider a fetus viable?" I asked.

He shrugged.

"When it graduates medical school."

Relieved that I hadn't uttered a blasphemy, Rabbi Friedman let out a small gale of air and laughed from the gut. If the Ba'al Shem Tov said God was also in every blade of grass, maybe He was even in every honest laugh. Maybe.

"Now I really need you to bring whatever you have in the way of tefillin," Rabbi Friedman said after dinner as I prepared to leave.

"Okay, I found my old pair, but they were beaten all to hel—I mean Gehenna," I said. Rabbi Friedman and I studied each other mutely.

I had stopped thinking about my own obsessions and turned back to why Rabbi Friedman had invited me in the first place. I had to learn to keep listening better, like he did, not chatter like the rabbis I'd known.

11

FATHERS AND SONS

A king's son once went astray from his father. The king sent a messenger to order the son to return home. The young man angrily refused, saying, "I can not." Finally, the king sent another emissary. This time, the message from his father was, "Return as far as you can—and I will come to you."

—the Talmud

I'd come to the Friedmans' door earlier for our sixth meeting. As he'd counseled, I'd self-consciously spent the last several weeks trying to reconnect with the father I'd purposefully pulled away from two decades before. I had amends to make, and at first the process was difficult.

"Sometimes your parents can't say what they mean, but they miss you, feel incomplete without you," Rabbi Friedman had told me. "They just can't say it, it gets stuck in their throats. So keep a ledger of the good and bad about them, and think about the good."

He's a good father, I reminded myself as I dialed the phone to his office, and he was. If parents sometimes get things they want to say to their children stuck in their craws, so it goes, too, for sons.

"Hello?" he said.

"Um," I said, my craw frozen.

"You all right?" he asked.

Completely out of context I began a Jewish doctor one-liner from

Henny Youngman. "A guy goes to his Jewish doctor," I said, "bends his arm so his elbow is pointing outward, and says, 'Doc, it hurts when I do this. What do you recommend?' "

"Don't do that!" he said, giving back the right punch line.

We both laughed.

"Vos macht a Yid?" (How you doing?) I asked. He'd always gotten a kick out of my Yiddish when I began studying it in college, and I always got a kick out of him getting a kick out of my speaking the language he used at home growing up. Half marveling at my lost cynicism, I realized I *did* still care.

"Zehr gut, vi gehts?" (Very well, what are you up to?)

"Gornisht, bupkes" (Nothing, zero), I said. "I was just thinking I haven't been over for a Friday night dinner in a while." Indeed, it must have been years since I'd last been back for one of those family affairs of yarmulkes, prayers, candles, wine, chicken, soup with homemade matzo balls, conversation about world affairs, gossip about the neighbors, one-liners, jokes about how my parents were still married because the divorce hadn't worked out.

"Sounds good," he said, as if I'd just been over last Friday. "Let me talk to your mother and sister."

"Don't let anybody cook," I said. "I'll bring kosher stuff home."

And I did. The first step had been taken.

A few weeks later I'd even given my father a subscription for his birthday to the English language version of New York's *Jewish Forward,* my grandfather's beloved *Forverts,* which still had columns about the speaking and meaning of Yiddish, as well as news of political infighting among Jewish groups and the actual dirt of what was going on nationally, be it rabbis being forced to resign from their high posts because of sins of the flesh or because they'd hired a hit man to kill their wife.

He loved it and would often send me *Forward* articles and book reviews he'd clipped from culture sections about Jewish gangsters, especially Meyer Lansky; Jewish athletes, especially Sandy Koufax; and Jewish rockers, especially Bob Dylan, all of whom regularly showed up in print.

For no particular reason except to show Rabbi Friedman I hadn't been a complete novice when I'd arrived on his doorstep, I'd also brought a satchelful of Jewish-related books, including some Hebraic texts from the early 1900s I'd dug out of a drawer in my old room at my parents' house during the week.

Dressing now to show respect, I was wearing a yarmulke, which I'd begun keeping in the glove compartment of my car. I was also wearing a tie and my only dress overcoat, and had traded in my jeans for slacks.

I had clung to my tefillin by not bringing them, though, honestly, I thought, not able to get home in time to pick them up for our meeting after he pressed me. In truth I just wasn't ready for any kind of hocus-pocus he was going to perform on my grandfather's beloved legacy. He hadn't said a word since, which I later learned was part of his philosophy of teaching.

Ever since I'd first read about the biblical *ger,* and the stranger's hope for redemption, I'd felt hope again. Even if Rabbi Friedman wasn't a wizard, and I didn't think he was, I felt I was going to begin what I imagined would be the long and winding adventure to reclaiming my *Yiddishe hartz.* Now, I heartily pushed the bell.

Rabbi Friedman himself opened the door. As he hung up my dress jacket, he nodded toward my open bag, overflowing with books, some not his own. "You're still studying Torah?" he asked.

I nodded. "A little. Warming up. And just like you told me, still just the Torah."

"The Torah is kind, that's good you're going back to it," he said. "You have not been kind to yourself, and that's not what God wants."

Over time I was learning to practice matching him silence for silence. I'd rarely heard such silence, such meaningful-*sounding* silence, in the presence of the pontificating rabbis who'd filled my former life. I now wanted to know who exactly this guy was I wanted to help me. Any cub reporter knows that to learn how a person grew up is to know in large part how he got to be where he is now. And a good interviewer knows that in time anyone will tell his story.

I'd told my students that all people want to tell their story. "All they have to be convinced of us is that you are sympathetic to them, paying attention, and know from doing your homework details of their lives no one seems to care about."

"My family was banished to Siberia from the interior of Russia during World War Two," Rabbi Friedman said, with the enthusiasm of someone reading a menu with nothing on it that he wanted to eat. He felt better, it seemed, when *others* were giving up the facts. "As it turned out," he continued, "Siberia was a far safer place to be than anywhere else in Eastern Europe.

"I was born in a Prague displaced-persons camp, and stayed there with my family until I was five, when we came to Brooklyn," he went on.

"Were you Hasidic?"

"No, Orthodox. There were thirteen people in my immediate family, and we all became Hasidic."

"Why?"

"My father worked as a bus driver to support us all, and we were poor. We lived in an apartment under street level, and all I saw of the world growing up were people's feet." He was silent for a bit.

"I was a wild child and a terrible student," he remembered.

He went to his bookshelf and pulled out a heavy leather-bound book composed entirely of pictures taken over the previous decades of Rebbe Schneerson marrying Hasidic couples under a wedding canopy.

"Are you in there?" I asked.

"Just one picture."

He turned to a page where a bespectacled young boy is running away from the canopy, literally *fleeing* from the rebbe. "It hadn't kicked in yet. It took me until sixteen for it to kick in," Rabbi Friedman repeated. "It sounds like it kicked in for you in a different way years earlier than for me."

Wow.

"Well, I was always pretty observant and devout growing up. I knew my stuff and cared until something kicked *out* of me," I said.

I understood in that moment that we were each drawn to the inverse equation between us.

The fact that Judaism kicked in for him late, and got knocked out of me around the same time, seemed to bind us like opposing magnets—we both had seen the other side, but from the other sides of our lives.

"When do you think your Judaism kicked out for you?" he asked, literally reading my mind.

I thought back. It had kicked out seven years before, when I saw at my wedding two simultaneously broken faces of people I loved: my wife and my father.

"But it must have happened before," he said. "From your background, to lose your sense of Judaism so completely that you apparently tried to assimilate and marry a non-Jewish woman just to get away—what caused *that*? That doesn't happen overnight."

He was right. It wasn't just that I decided to assimilate as quickly and thoroughly as possible a decade before I got married. "I think," I said truthfully, "it happened in stages. Or maybe all at once. Or never."

"Or always," he said, smiling.

He nodded toward the books I'd brought from my parents' home and had put out on the table. There were two different versions of the Torah, and a siddur, a tiny prayer book from Israel that my grandfather had given me before he died when I was fourteen. I'd brought along only miniature paper copies of the Torah, good for practicing from; the holy book of Revealed Law he'd wanted me to study; plus an Orthodox prayer book without a word of English in it from the turn of the century. I'd practiced hard during the previous week. I wanted to show him my willingness to apply myself to scholarship by quickly removing the barnacles from my Hebrew education.

I'd started work on the story of Abraham and Isaac, the father willing to kill the son for the Jewish God.

When I'd started studying, sounding out the words from the Hebrew text, the language under my fingertips, long lost to my tongue, had come out of my mouth tortured, haltingly, and shrill.

Yet I'd worked at it, and surprisingly pronunciations came back fairly quickly. I was once again reading and speaking the ancient Hebrew and Aramaic of the Torah. Genesis, Exodus, Leviticus, Numbers, and Deuteronomy were no longer the Five Books of Moses; once again I knew them by their Hebrew names, the ones taken from one of the first few words of each book: *Braysheet, Sh'mute, Va-yee-kra, Ba'meed-bar, D'varim.*

Now, at Rabbi Friedman's, I took out the copy of the generations-old Hebrew Bible that my grandfather had given to me. I also lifted out my old and battered Tikkun, its cover falling off. The volume, a severe-looking, oversized, black hardcover book with two columns of Hebrew on each page, was used by Torah readers to learn and practice their public readings, and to tutor kids for their bar or bat mitzvahs.

I hadn't used it to practice reading Torah since my last semester of college. It was right around then that I'd also told my father that, come to think of it, I wasn't going to be a rabbi after all and study the Eternal, but was going to New York to work at a magazine to write about the previous week's news.

Out of this book I'd tutored dozens of twelve-year-olds for their bar or bat mitzvahs. Weirdly, I'd never once in my life wondered why this practical book and tool for Torah readers was called a "Tikkun," "heal," like *tikkun olam* (heal the world).

When I'd told my father the bad news about rabbinical school, he said a few words of his own and even tried to make a joke, using a saying of my Yiddish grandfather: "Vat vaz vaz, vat iz iz, and datz dat."

"*That's* where my Judaism really crumbled forever," I said, "with that *look.*"

"Why do you think it took so long to realize that somewhere

along the line your Judaism had disappeared?'" Rabbi Friedman asked. After all, it was seven years since the divorce, almost twenty since I'd tossed away Judaism. Wouldn't I have been at least conscious of my despair long before?

I thought of Hemingway. "'He was awake a long time,'" I quoted, "'before he remembered his heart was broken.'"

Tikkun olam, heal the world. *Tikkun mein Yiddishe hartz,* heal my Jewish heart. "I thought *tikkun olam* was the point of the Kabbalah." I asked, just out of curiosity.

"Well, there's been a lot of *talk* about that being said there," he said, dummying up, as he was supposed to, discouraging spiritual wanderers, those not qualified to study the Kabbalah, which was virtually everyone in the world including me, from poking around too much. "I don't know if the Kabbalah even uses that expression."

Right. I found I was beginning to enjoy the verbal volleying, like Felix and Oscar in *The Odd Couple.*

"Rabbi," I said, "you know I'm not looking for Madonna's Kabbalah Lite, and that I'm smart enough to know I'm not smart enough to start learning the real Kabbalah. But there are a lot of people who say *everything* is explained in the Kabbalah. There are scholars who say everything *you* believe in is in the Kabbalah."

"No," Rabbi Friedman said strongly. "You have to combine everything, all the texts. The Torah says something here, the Talmud mentions something there, the Kabbalah talks of something else somewhere else."

"Can you give me one example, and then I'll shut up?"

He sighed. "Okay," he said, "let's discuss humility. With humility comes the shrinking of the self, and one can more easily deal with the spiritual matters of making yourself better in an overwhelming world."

"Understood," I said.

"Well, take Pesach, when the Jews were led out of bondage, and Shavuos, when they received the Ten Commandments seven weeks later and the harvest celebrating that we can take care of ourselves after being in slavery. The Torah says to count each of those days, the counting of the Omer. Meantime, the Kabbalah says that in the counting of the Omer, we go through seven weeks where each week we're supposed to look at one of the seven human emotions and see how we can each improve."

"Count the days?" I asked. "Emotions?"

"Here's something you need to know about the Kabbalah, even if you never intend to be a kabbalist—kindness, severity, and compassion. Those three emotions are excitement. We get excited and spirited by love, fear, and compassion. Every great book must be about one or all of those three subjects.

"Those emotions are what provide us with the drama that animates our lives. Every human relationship starts off with these three emotions. In Hebrew they are *chesed, gevura,* and *teferess.*

"Then there are the next three emotions," he continued. "They're not exciting or inspired, but kind of dull and dry. But they're more reliable. You can be moved by love, but that in itself won't last forever—these next emotions are about whether you will still be able to be loving when the inspiration is gone."

"What would happen after the romantic movie is over," I said, "and the couple actually had to go on."

"Exactly. These second three emotions are about *continuing,* to persevere, to see your task through. Now, you may suspect someone doesn't love you, but that's not necessarily true. Because the ability to *act* on love comes not from love itself—but from *netz-ach,* the fourth emotion.

"The fourth emotion tells a person about the one he once fell in love with what he should feel. *Netz-ach* is really telling people to think about their mates, 'Okay, I'm not so excited by you anymore as I once was. But *you're* the one. So here's the kindness, here's the love, as always.' "

"Number five?" I asked, wondering when true humility would be entering the equation.

"That's called *chod,* discipline. People talk about others who can't lose a hundred pounds and say, 'They don't really want to lose that weight.' Not true. They probably mean it a hundred percent, but something is missing, the fifth emotion—*chod*."

"I was never much into having to show discipline," I said.

"Yes," he continued, "but for the kindness and love, the first three emotions, you need a backup, a see-it-through emotion. And so discipline—some might call it even fear—provides that backup to make it happen. That fifth emotion is what keeps us sane. If we had only the exciting emotions we'd be totally crazy, because by their very definition, you don't know what's going to happen next with exciting emotions. With excitement, you can be up one moment and down the next. So to have a relationship that lasts more than three hours we need this second set of emotions."

"So what is the next set *about*?"

"It's about the other person, not you. The first emotions are all about me. I get excited about things that are mine. My love is about me, even if I love you. It's real love, but it's still about me. The next three emotions aren't about me. They come from circumstance. So you say, 'I used to love you, I was very excited, now I'm not so excited, but you are my wife, so I continue to act accordingly.' "

"And that's humility?" I asked.

"Yes. The first three emotions are energy, the second three are humility. Why do we need three levels of humility? Because there are three distinct types. We've talked about *netz-ach*—'I will see it through, it has to happen, it's got to be.' It comes from the outside situation, not myself, my ability to put myself aside and focus on what is called for. I can leave my feelings and respond. I can't stop until it's done. If it were my personal issue, I'd get tired, bored, and quit in the middle. If it were just about, and up to, me, I'd do it halfway, and say that's good enough."

"Can you give an example?"

"Okay," he said. "The previous rebbe's son was sent by his father on a mission to destroy a manuscript an anti-Semitic professor was going to hand over to the czar about some terrible things Jews had supposedly done. Pogroms would result if it were published, and the previous rebbe's son, who was a young man at the time, went to see what he could do.

"So the son met the anti-Semitic professor and argued with him. He reasoned, threatened, even tried to bribe him for the manuscript, but nothing worked. So he went back to his father, who was putting on his tallis and about to daven [pray], and said, 'I couldn't accomplish anything.' His father said there was no such thing.

"So the son went back and asked the professor if he could at least see the manuscript. And the anti-Semite, in his arrogance and his pride in himself for the damage he would soon be causing, took the book out to lord over the rebbe's son. And before he could respond, the son snatched the manuscript and tore it up, destroyed it. The professor of course lost his temper and hit the son, but the damage was done—it would take him years to redo it. This was before Zip drives.

"When he got back to his father and told him what had happened, his father said, '*A potch gekregen oder gesacht oys gefehrt*'—You got slapped but accomplished what you had to accomplish. Now, that's *netz-ach*."

"I like that," I said. "Ya gotta do what ya gotta do. What's number five?"

"That's called *ha-da-ah* and is also called gratitude. It is an acknowledgment, on a deeper level of humility, where you are able to say, 'I am insignificant, but you are not.' "

"Isn't that codependence?" I asked.

"No," he said, though I wasn't sure if he knew the word. "Gratitude, or recognition or acknowledgment, is the ability to attribute significance to someone beyond ourselves. When we attribute significance to our ancestors, our people, our nation, God—that is a deeper humility."

"Anything else?"

"The third level of humility is called *y'sode*. It's related to reproduction, but it's actually self-sacrifice. It's to die so that someone else can live. Every parent dies a little bit to give life to his or her children. Those are the three levels of humility."

A couple of days later, I was looking at a poster of the tree of life, the Kabbalah's Atz Chaim, which spells out in Hebrew the ten *sefirot*, the levels from earth to heaven that must be bridged before *tikkun olam* can heal the world and bring together the male and female aspects of God.

The first six levels were named *chesed, gevura, teferess, net-zach, chod,* and *y'sode*. I'd had an in-depth Kabbalah lesson, shrouded in a talk about Shavuos, and barely knew it.

"And what does this have to do with healing the world?" I asked.

He still didn't say if *tikkun olam* was even in the Kabbalah.

"Now God fits into this idea in one of two ways. Either *tikkun olam* means making the world good for people, socially good. Looking at it that way, God's role is to help and instruct us. The other possibility is that *tikkun olam* doesn't mean healing the world for the good of people, but for the good of God. He needs us to keep kosher, as much as we need to keep it; and just as we need a good life and good world, God needs it even more. So really this belief doesn't mean 'heal the world,' it means 'make the world godly.' And godly means the world has been healed for God. That's the punch line."

"But in the process," I asked, "is there something called *tikkun . . .* Help me out," I said, *"tikkun a'ni?* Heal me? Or doesn't that even matter?"

"Healing oneself is part of what God wants," he said. "It's just not an end in itself. Once we find out what kind of world appeals to God, it turns out His kind of world is good for human beings. We really end up with a good world in the simple sense and a world that is godly. So we need to have a society that follows the Ten Commandments, where people don't kill each other, and He needs that even more. What His purposes are, we have no idea."

I'd read this about the Hasidim. Supposedly they believe that only about a tenth of what life actually consists of is apparent, be it in your face or a newspaper's reality. The rest is hidden, unfathomable or unseeable to the human eye or brain. But each mitzvah done by each person brings God's purpose one step closer to fruition.

Then again, I didn't believe in God.

I should have guessed what was coming next, knowing that my personally performing mitzvoth, the commandments in the Torah, whether I believed in them or not, was considered by these people as bringing the entire world one step closer to salvation.

12

SPIRITUAL AIRPORTS

Rabbi Friedman had been giving me a pass for a long time on bringing in my tefillin. But no more. "Okay," he said, "you'll need tefillin, like I said when we first met here."

"Okay," I said.

I had my grandfather's one-hundred-year-old tefillin, which he'd brought over with his wine press from Russia. I also had the tefillin my grandfather had given me for my bar mitzvah, and which I first wore at camp.

"Bring both pairs in," Friedman said. "We have to see if either are still kosher."

"I didn't know tefillin could *be* kosher. And if they aren't?"

"Then you'll have to buy a pair. They're the only thing you'll have to buy, but I have a cousin in Crown Heights. They're expensive, sometimes a thousand dollars for a good pair, but I'll see what he can do."

Whoa. A thousand bucks. Here's where it begins, I thought, the shakedowns I'd always heard the Lubavitch were famous for. I didn't know if I could scrape it together.

"Don't worry about that. If you never pay him, he'll send them anyway," Rabbi Friedman reassured me, "because he can't stand the thought of a Jew not having tefillin."

Well, that was better.

"One thing," I asked. "We talked about the tug of Cain versus Abel. But after going back to that Torah portion, I realize I really am still in exile like Cain here, with nowhere to go or go back to, even to my own Judaism."

"Hmmm. So what makes this exile? You're from here originally."

"It's a spiritual thing, a *feeling* thing. Like I'm at the wrong airport and don't know where I'm supposed to be going."

"Not necessarily," he said. "Let's say you *are* at the airport. But let's take the airport in a *Jewish* context. The Twin Cities airport is the hub for Northwest Airlines. Everywhere I go, it's usually on Northwest. So if somebody says, 'Why don't you take Southwest Airlines?' I say, 'I'm sure it's a wonderful airline, it takes you where you want to go, which is Florida. But I want to go to New York.'"

"I'm not sure if I get your point," I said.

"It's the *destination* we're talking about, and the destination for me is Judaism. Everybody talks about the 'true religion.' As far as I'm concerned, every religion is 'true.' If I were interested in enlightenment, my destination would be Buddhism, and I'd have to fly another airline, maybe switch planes to another hub. If my destination were heaven, safe from Satan, my destination would be Christianity."

"So each religion has a different point?" I interjected. "A different God? A Buddhist, Islamic, Christian, Jewish, whatever God?"

"No. But we look for Him in different ways, often the wrong ways. It all depends on our destinations, where we've been and are going to, with all our connections to the past and the generations coming."

He laughed. "You know, I recently ran into a Jewish boy whom I hadn't seen in many years. He was all grown up now, and I asked, 'How've you been? What's going on?'

"And he said, 'Oh, I've become a Buddhist.' I asked him how come, and he said, 'To get closer to God—isn't that great?'

"And I said, 'Well that's nice, but how do you know that He wants you any closer? Maybe you're close enough. Maybe you've gotten too close and He needs you to back off a little bit, because you're cramping His style.' "

The story was funny, but I still couldn't see my own situation clearly.

"Look," he said, "it's not necessary for you to suffer and worry like this. Let me tell you a story."

Good. I was a scholar, collecting wisdom. He, meantime, seemed to be dangling metaphysical and practical hints and notions, sometimes named, sometimes not, as carrots to keep me interested, or at least reading the Torah portion every week. His main message seemed to be *relax.* We can follow the captain's orders, but we aren't steering the boat.

"One day, word spread that the previous rebbe's uncle's forest had burned down and his life savings lost," Rabbi Friedman began. I settled into my chair and smiled. I enjoyed his stories and shaggy dog delivery. It reminded me of the old Myron Cohen vinyl records my parents had of gentle comic Jewish stories told in a deep Yiddish accent.

"So some friends rushed over to his house to console the previous rebbe's uncle about the fire. When they got there they found him quietly reading. They figured he hadn't heard yet, and when they finally told him he said, 'I heard an hour ago.' "

"They said, 'You knew? When we got here you were casually reading a book. Weren't you upset?'

" 'Of course I was upset,' he said. 'But that was an hour ago.' He then turned to one of his friends and asked, 'How come you're not upset about your kid not being well?'

" 'I was upset,' his friend said, 'but that was three years ago, and I got over it.'

"So the previous rebbe's uncle said, 'Okay, by you it takes three years, by me it takes an hour. So I'm faster than you. And if you know in three years you won't be upset, why be upset now? It's the problems that won't go away you worry about. I could be upset for ten years about a fire, but why wait? Why not go for the minimum?' "

The end.

"Yes?" I asked.

"So what are you so worried about? Why not go for the minimum of worrying and wondering who you really are and what the point of your life is?"

"But what if the problem isn't about time, but life?" I asked solipsistically. "What about life running out, unlived?"

He shook his head. "The purpose of life is the absolute conviction that when God creates human beings, He doesn't do it in masses. The point is that we are individuals, able to do those mitzvoth in the Torah, for God, our own way, the best we can.

"The most important lesson in the entire story of Creation isn't that God created dark and light or grass and stars, or that He put the planets in their orbits. What's important is that God created one person. That more than anything else sets the tone of our life. He creates only individuals. The world is partly good and partly evil; our purpose is to guard the good and to work to improve what is evil. It gets much more complicated, especially if you want to spend years studying Kabbalah and trying to figure out what God gets out of all that He's made. But basically, that's the meaning of life."

"That's it?" I said.

"And the basic question of *Judaism* . . ." he began, seeing if I remembered.

"Is can Jews get along," I responded.

"And . . .?"

"No," I answered.

We both laughed, really laughed. As usual.

"Manis and Nissan," Chana said, appearing in the doorway, "Moitel and Chaya are here, dinner's ready."

I put away my books, Rabbi Friedman rose, and we walked out of the office to the living room where his son and daughter-in-law were hanging their coats. I asked each how they were. *"Baruch HaShem,"* they each said, with a broad welcoming smile that made me feel a nearby cousin if not exactly a member of the immediate family. In this *haimish* atmosphere, I felt warm, innocent, and guileless.

"Come," Rabbi Friedman said, "let's wash."

I couldn't remember the last time anybody expected me as a matter of course to stay for dinner. When I'd leave afterward, I often couldn't remember exactly what Rabbi Friedman and I had discussed about the Torah, if anything—*Baruch HaShem,* I had my tape recorder.

Rather, what I remembered was the warmth of that elongated table that sometimes sat two and sometimes fourteen for dinner; the industrial-strength horseradish I'd piled on, clearing my nose and cranium and sending me wheezing, as people slapped my back in good-hearted laughter. The jokes.

Weirdly, there had been a turnaround. Not long before, it was Judaism I loved but Jews I couldn't stand. Now I disagreed heartily with much of the Judaism of these people—but I liked them *as* Jews, *because* they were Jews.

At the dinner table he questioned me about my life (not much to report), pounded out *nigguns* next to my elbow, and asked about the baseball race. A stand-up guy. I wasn't used to wanting to hang around guys, stand-up or not, who wanted me to hang around their families. Now, I realized, here I wasn't a *ger.* I was a member of a community, even if I refused to join.

We went to the sink and poured a cup of water over each of our hands. Everything, I would later learn from Rabbi Friedman, was Kabbalistic-centered: The ten washed fingers symbolized the ten *sefirot,* the levels that separated earth, which was overseen by God's bride, the *Shkeinah.*

At the moment, however, all I thought I was doing was washing my hands before dinner and repeating after Rabbi Friedman a prayer I used to know, not symbolically cleansing the ten-step ladder up to God in heaven. Not even my ignorance mattered; performing the mitzvah, the good deed, was the thing—belief in it (*kavanah*) could come or not. "God doesn't want us to do mitzvoth," Friedman said, "He *needs* us to."

"So why does He need us to wash our hands before eating? Hygiene, or because it's an unexplained commandment in the Torah?"

"It's beyond our comprehension," Rabbi Friedman said, "and we'll never know. All we are is human."

"*A mentsch is nebekh, nit mer vi a mentsch un amol dos oykh nit*" (A person is only a person—and sometimes not even that), I said, finishing a Yiddish idiom I'd learned growing up.

Rabbi Friedman sat at the head of the table, and I sat next to him. Alongside me was his son, Rabbi Mordchai "Moitel" Friedman, thirty-one. The little kids—Nissan and Muschka—sat at the end, while in between was another son, Rabbi Eli Friedman, visiting from New York. Near the end of the table was a former Minneapolis resident visiting from New York. He was a jovial, middle-aged *Ba'al teshuva*—a previously assimilated Jew who'd converted to Hasidism—who I was pleased to see could read Hebrew about a tenth as well as I could. But his passion was evident.

Moitel had arrived looking exhausted from a long day running the country's only yeshiva for at-risk Lubavitch youth. "At risk for what?" I asked.

"Leaving Lubavitch," he said. "And for everything else American teenagers are at risk for."

"Drugs? Rock and roll?" I asked facetiously.

He gave me an Ann Landers wake-up-and-smell-the-coffee look. Across the table his wife, Chaya, sat dandling their baby. Theirs was a Hasidic royal fairy tale. Moitel Friedman, the young but already seasoned rabbi son of the esteemed Rabbi Manis Friedman, had won, a couple of years before, the hand of Chaya Kagan, twenty-one, widely considered the most beautiful woman in all Hasidim.

She was also the daughter of the Detroit scholar Rabbi Yitzchak Meier Kagan. Rabbi Kagan was embarked on his life's work—translating into English the late Rebbe Schneerson's intricate and scholarly Yiddish elucidations upon the Torah and Talmud commentaries given by Rashi. It would be a commentary on a commentary on a commentary on the Torah. "Rabbi Kagan has a beautiful pen," Friedman said approvingly of the monumental task under way by his daughter-in-law's father. "He's the right man for the job."

After some prayers, a dinner of chicken soup, gefilte fish, and chicken was served, and once again, the meal was interrupted several times by wordless singsong *nigguns* that erupted spontaneously and the fist poundings. As he led his family into and out of the melodies, Rabbi Friedman closed his eyes, seemingly in rapture. Without thinking, I began pounding along to a *niggun* for the first time in a generation, la-la-ing one note behind the melody.

Community. Family. It seemed like some sort of template for *something*.

Between eating and banging, the unlikely topic at hand seemed to be the Hasids' favorite Steven Wright jokes.

"I have a house next door to the airport," Moitel said. "I went from the living room to the dining room, and a flight attendant told me to sit down."

"I've found I never have problems at airport check-in," the *Ba'al teshuva* interjected with a piece of practical advice, "if I bring a salami and give it to the reservations agent. No one ever gives them anything but grief."

"Good idea," said Rabbi Friedman, then returned to Steven Wright. "I was stopped at the border, and the guard said, 'Do you have any weapons?' I said, 'What do you need?'"

"What, no jokes tonight, no jokes anymore?" Moitel asked me in the midst of the shtick fest. "Getting serious?"

I ignored the question and racked my memory for a Steven Wright one-liner of my own. All I could come up with was, "You can't have everything. Where would you put it?"

It was then that I realized that these one-liners weren't shtick. They were an excuse to feel and share innocent pleasure, they were innocent joy.

I'd been so attracted to shtick all these years for different reasons. I'd traded in my Judaism—as well as my tefillin, not to mention the teachings of Torah meant to turn one toward menschhood—for the kind of assimilation and camaraderie I thought I could win as an American. An American using my Jewish-based shtick, where nobody on the outside could see my empty husk of self-loathing.

The tug. I didn't want to be like old-world Charlie Chan with his Asian wise man movie aphorisms: "Mind like umbrella, only work when open."

This was honest joy. I could be me, that's all they wanted.

For the first time in two decades I felt as if it was *possible* for me to become what I'd been: a Jew who considers himself a real Jew, by his own standards.

Before I left, I wondered aloud to Rabbi Friedman if he thought I was kind of pathetic just on the grounds I was forty, divorced from a gentile, with no kids. I felt like a freak about it in the secular world, among Jews and gentiles; among the Lubavitch, I should have been on the verge of having grandchildren.

He shook his head and offered one last piece of advice. "You're *still* on the rebound," he said, turning the focus again, I thought, to my long-past marriage.

On the rebound.

I remembered my basketball coach freshman year of high school, the one who always called the Hebrew school I was forced to attend and forever miss practices for "religion," as in, "You got religion today, Karlen?"

I also remembered how much he talked about the holiness of rebounds, how you had to follow your shots, because even if you missed, you might be able to rebound the ball off the backboard or hoop and start all over again.

Driving home, however, the old doubts began creeping in. But now I was forty, and for roughly two decades I hadn't been following my shots and trying to rebound my own misfires. Like a basketball headed inexorably out of bounds, evading the scramble of bodies and hands around it, nothing had held on to me, and I had held on to nothing.

13

TEFILLIN AND THE ART OF SANDY KOUFAX

God, too, wears tefillin.
            —the Kabbalah

Yom Kippur is the holiest day of the Jewish religion. The [team] knows that I don't work that day. I'm Jewish. I'm a role model. I want [Jews] to understand they have to have pride.
            —Sandy Koufax's explanation of why he, a nonobservant Jew, didn't pitch the opening game of the 1965 World Series for the Los Angeles Dodgers in Minneapolis against the Minnesota Twins

A couple of days before our next visit, I realized that in the previous month the nightmares had ceased. That minor miracle—the regrets were still there, but I didn't have to sit through a quadruple feature every night showing my fuckups and transgressions—gave me faith. *T'shuva.* I was indeed turning.

So, giving Friedman credit, I decided finally to stop being a schmuck and just bring in my tefillin. I'd overcome my reflexive senses of embarrassment at the very notion of wearing them and doing *that* whenever a rabbi said do *this.*

I would play along.

"Did you bring your tefillin?" Rabbi Friedman asked first thing the next time I was in the door. I handed him two bags and went into the study and found my usual seat, where I shifted uncomfortably. I thought of the mitzvah-mobiles—the RVs the Lubavitch would park on Fifth Avenue and shanghai men who'd admitted they were Jews inside to put on tefillin. I wondered if that Hasid who had accosted me with the question, "You a Jew?" way back when had been right.

"So what's the big deal about tefillin?" I asked.

He explained patiently. Since they were portable, you could wear them anywhere, announcing to the world you weren't afraid to say you're a Jew.

"It's also the only commandment that encompasses the heart, the mind, and the arm," he said. "The *tefillin shel rosh* [of the head] are a *keter* [crown] around your head that encompasses your thoughts. The one around your arm must be worn on the biceps, and symbolizes strength. And while standing in prayer, the box on your arm must touch the side of your chest—your heart."

Aha. So the tefillin connected one's heart, head, and muscle. This I liked.

I looked warily at the X-Acto knife Rabbi Friedman was holding inches from my grandfather's century-old tefillin boxes that my father had dug out of some bureau drawer for me.

I had barely sat down when Rabbi Friedman immediately said, "Let's see what you've got."

Along with my grandfather's sacramental wine press, these tefillin, in their faded and cinched blue bag with the long-ago stitched-on Hebrew word "God" inside a Jewish star, were the most precious things he owned. He'd wrapped them on his head and arm every morning as he prayed for the seventy-four years after *his* grandfather gave them to him at *his* bar mitzvah. He didn't stop until the very day of his fatal heart attack in the tiny Orthodox shul he walked to three times a day.

"Are you *sure* you have to do that?" I said, sagging, as he prepared to slice into the leather.

He was good with the blade, like a medical examiner about to perform just another autopsy on someone he didn't know. Seeing me blanch as the knife neared the largest of the tefillin's three boxes, he tried to reassure me that he knew what he was doing. Before he'd become a rabbi, he said, "I was going to become a *sofer* [ritual scribe for Torahs, mezuzot, and tefillin]."

I shifted uncomfortably and stared at the knife's point and then my grandfather's prayer boxes. "Your *zayda* took very good care to make sure these tefillin stayed kosher," he said, inspecting them like a diamond cutter spying angles of approach. "These boxes still have perfectly squared corners. If the corners had been rounded, it would mean they'd been misused or worn down. They'd be *trayf* and worthless."

Worthless? My Orthodox grandfather's century-old, meticulously used, loved and taken care of tefillin? I felt Rabbi Friedman was being a little cavalier, especially considering how he'd preached to me about the care with which holy items must be handled. Even worn-out prayer books aren't thrown away but ritually buried like any person who'd lived a proper Jewish life. The world was created with words, I knew the Hasidim believed, and I couldn't figure out why he seemed so indifferent to this other holder of some of God's most important decrees, my grandfather's tefillin.

"Before you do that," I said, holding his arm to stop the knife, "can I ask you something?"

"Sure."

"I know that the only mitzvah mentioned four times in the Torah is putting on tefillin. But why are there so many other mentions of it in the Oral Law, like seemingly every Mishnah, Talmudic tract, Gemara, whatever, has a quote about tefillin?"

"Look," he said, "the Oral Torah is our special gift that all the people with the Bible don't have. It was given to Moses by God on Mount Sinai with the written Torah, which of course is our version of Scripture. But without the Oral Law, the Written Law is misunderstood, poisoned, misapplied, it just doesn't work. We need the Oral Law of the Gemara, the Talmud, the Mishnah," he enumerated, listing some of the commentaries and explanations of the Torah written down in the first several centuries after Jesus.

"Isn't there more danger of people misunderstanding the Bible if everything *isn't* written down?" I asked, deciding not to push it. "And anyway, all that oral stuff *was* eventually written down."

"But not for a long time after it was given to Moses," he said. "If you keep passing something down orally through the generations, you keep it alive. You can't just put it on your shelf and forget about it. Even people who believe in the Bible have never read it cover to cover, and if they have, they don't know what they've read. But if you have to memorize it, make people *live* with it in their heads—well, that's a very valid reason for keeping all the juicy stuff oral."

"Juicy stuff?"

"They're *all* part of the Oral Law," he said.

"But why is this Oral Law so important if we already had the Torah written down? What about the elbow room the Kabbalah supposedly gives you to define Judaism?"

"Definitions can always change, depending on your study of the Oral Law."

"Like?" I said.

Rabbi Friedman stood up and walked to one of his bookcases. "Let's talk about relationships." He reached up and took down a book written in Hebrew.

"Here," he said, "the first Mishnah, Chapter One."

I read the Hebrew script. *"Vi-all tar-bay seem-ach ihm awl ha'eeshah,"* I said aloud.

"At first glance this says, 'Do not talk too much to *the* woman,' " he said. "But if you look closely, it says *tar-bay,* which means 'overmuch,' not *har-bay,* which means 'talk too much to *a* woman.' "

"What's the difference?" I said.

"Big difference. All *'tar-bay seem-ach'* means is don't create conversation with a woman after you said what you've had to say. Literally it means 'make talk.' Men don't talk to men when they don't have anything to say, but they tend to do that with women. Why? Because he doesn't think of her as *a* woman, but *the* woman—he objectifies her. Here you see how the Mishnah from all these centuries ago was dealing with a concept—objectifying women—that didn't even have a name in the dictionary fifty years ago."

"Smart Mishnah," I said.

"However," he went on, "the Mishnah is also not saying put women on pedestals—just that if you wouldn't say something to a man, don't say it to a woman. Your attitude toward *a* woman has to be respectful—including your own wife."

"And . . . ?"

"The Mishnah is imprecise in its language here, so you have to be able to interpret it yourself, and live accordingly. It's all Torah."

Rabbi Friedman then picked up his X-Acto knife again and prepared to dig into my grandfather's tefillin. I still wasn't ready.

"Can I tell *you* an ancient story about rabbis that kind of explains how I feel about what you're doing?" I asked. "I think it's even kind of funny."

"Fine." He put down the knife, looking pleased that I now wanted to tell tales of Jewish rabbis instead of one-liners about Jewish noses.

"What's the Hasidic tradition?" I asked. "Do I start these stories with the conclusion, or the story itself?"

"However you want. Martin Buber didn't write *how* to tell *Tales of the Hasidim,* did he?" he asked, laughing at the man he considered the biggest shtickmeister of all.

"Okay," I began, trying to remember the story my father had told me years after I decided not to become ordained.

Now, sitting next to Rabbi Friedman's desk, delaying my story to stall the tefillin chopping, I thought I saw the fierce *mitnaggid* Aaron Karlen's horrified face as a Hasidic enemy took out his X-Acto knife to slice up the little black boxes he'd smuggled across Europe. He'd run away rather than be inducted into the army for the special twenty-year term reserved for shtetl Jews to make sure they assimilated—by never being allowed to eat kosher food, daven four times a day, or ever return to Karlin.

Who cared, I wondered silently, whether the tefillin were technically kosher? Wasn't the point that Aaron Karlen was enough of a mensch, had enough of a *Yiddishe* heart, to bring his tefillin to the new country? Suddenly, it felt as if I were thinking of my grandfather for the first time as a real person, a man with actual feelings and not just some old-world junk man who spent fifty years steadfastly refusing to assimilate.

Wasn't this just the kind of rigidity that had driven me away from my religion in the first place? For the first time I felt angry, truly mad, at Rabbi Friedman.

True, I'd never been moved by my *zayda*'s tefillin until shortly before this. But did that matter? The point, I thought, was that now I felt there was history, a past I hadn't cared one whit about, in those old phylacteries. In the end, though, I decided to let the rabbi have his way. In any case, I knew from his own Orthodoxy that my grandfather would be the first to toss them away if they didn't meet the strictest standards. And, after all, this ritual of wearing kosher tefillin was the only thing Rabbi Friedman had demanded of me.

"What are you thinking about? What about the funny story about the rabbi?" Friedman asked, picking up his scalpel again, poised. I felt like he was a doctor trying to distract a kid while giving him an injection.

"I'm thinking of my grandfather," I said. "How happy he'd be if his tefillin had survived a century, two worlds, and three generations, still kosher."

"He'd be proud of you, making sure his tefillin were still kosher a century after he got them. He sounds like he was a true tzaddik [righteous man]."

"That he was," I said desultorily.

The czar's army had earlier caught his older brother, who died in a German World War I prisoner of war camp. In response, my grandfather only made the overt gesture of marking his own past by naming my American-born father after my late great uncle with his exact name—Markle—rather than some more new-world variation. He insisted on always calling my father by his brother's shtetl name, a habit my father adopted his whole life, while I made fun of him to my friends by referring to my dad, Markle Karlen, as "Markle Karkel."

Then I was thinking of my grandfather hiding in hay bales and running through forests at night to stay Jewish, the tefillin in his pocket and wine press on his back. "You're spacing out," Rabbi Friedman said. "Tell me your story."

"Okay. A rabbinical student is about to leave Eastern Europe for a job in the United States. He goes to his rabbi, one of the great Talmudic sages of his time, and asks for any departing wisdom. 'Life is a fountain,' the rabbi tells the student.

"The student is deeply impressed by the profundity of this statement, and he leaves for a very successful career as a new-world rabbi. Thirty years later, he hears that his teacher is on his deathbed, and the younger man goes back for a last visit.

" 'Rabbi,' he says when he sees his mentor, 'may I ask you one question? Over the last thirty years, whenever I've been sad or depressed, I've thought of the words you told me right before I took off for the United States. They have helped me get through the most difficult of times. But to be truthful, Rabbi, I haven't ever really figured out what you meant. And now that you are about to go to *O'lam Ha'bah* [the world to come], maybe you could enlighten me as to what your words actually mean? Rabbi, why *is* life like a fountain?'

"The old rabbi looked up from his deathbed, exhausted. 'All right,' he says, 'so maybe life *isn't* like a fountain.' "

Friedman laughed. "Good story. And there's a ring of truth in there. We're living in a time when the whole world is looking for moral clarity, and the rabbis are doing nothing. Judaism's biggest problem is with the rabbis—many have this terrible pathology that they pass down, where they prefer to be victims than to stick up for what is right by Torah, right by life. They'd rather have Jews be killed and tortured as helpless beings—they're comfortable with that—than have Jews defend themselves on the grounds of being right."

"Right?" I asked.

"I've always wondered why there are no rabbis on television, like the televangelists," he said. "A lot of rabbis certainly like talking, hearing themselves deliver their own messages. When they come up to debate me after I give a talk, I say, 'Why don't you get a television show? You're handsome, you're smart, you believe in what you say, and it doesn't matter if what you say about Torah is true, the real *emes.*' "

Rabbi Friedman seemed to think even less of rabbis as a whole than I did.

I banged my hand on the table in mockery of a late-night televangelist and put on an exaggerated Yiddish accent. "You vant a Got?" I said. "Have we got a Got for you!" I *shpritzed* like the would-be comics at New York's Friars Club. "I always figured that if God decided to talk to us through the television, He'd at least get network time, not an infomercial."

"Let's take an example," he said. "Rabbis keep talking about Europe: What does Europe think of us, what does it think of Israel, what can we do to make Europe *like* the Jews? Europe! Who *cares* what Europe thinks of the Jews? They allowed the Holocaust to happen!"

"I know," I said, beginning to seethe.

He picked up the X-Acto and reached again for my grandfather's tefillin.

I still wasn't ready. "Where was our golem in World War Two, when my grandfather's family was being slaughtered?" I asked.

The rabbi remained mute and drummed his two index fingers on his desk. Suddenly, I was no longer just trying to stall but was filled with a hate and thirst for revenge that was scaring me.

Friedman stroked his beard and looked puzzled. "I've never seen you so angry," he said, not especially impressed.

Yet weirdly, that anger led me to a place where I'd never felt more Jewish, except for perhaps that moment after my wedding when I realized the woman I loved would never be on my side, whatever side that might be. That anger felt intoxicating—and very unmenschlike. This wasn't the form of spirituality I was seeking. As Tess Gallagher wrote, "If you're looking for revenge, dig two graves."

"You talk about this and that rabbi," I said, "but I feel a little like you're giving me mixed messages. Because of ritual, it's terrible to put a copy of Rashi's commentary on the Bible on the floor, but it's okay to nonchalantly cut into my grandfather's tefillin to see if they're worthless, to destroy the very thing that made him feel Jewish? I feel ashamed of myself, like I'm standing by while my own blood is being killed."

"If they aren't kosher," he explained simply, "they're just black straps and boxes with pieces of paper inside. And don't you remember one of the reasons I said why putting on *kosher* tefillin, is so important? Because you can do it outside, in an airport, in the middle of a football stadium. It's a way for us to get over our embarrassment of who we are."

"Okay," I said reluctantly. I still didn't like what he was going to do to my grandfather's tefillin, but I understood his point, and I thought once more of how the old man probably would have approved. Just because one might be on his or her way to a *Yiddishe* heart didn't make tefillin kosher. I was slowly beginning to learn the rules.

"Okay," he said. "Let's see."

———————

Taking up the knife again, he pried off what he identified from his studies as the kind of paraffin used to seal tefillin boxes made in Eastern Europe around the 1880s. Rabbi Friedman used tweezers to extract a couple of the four tiny handwritten parchments rolled up inside the black box. He then undid the barely visible black threads that kept the holy paper rolled up.

I watched, horrified at first. And then scared. Then entranced. So *that* was what was inside those boxes all these years.

"Back then they tied each piece of parchment with tiny horse-tail hairs," he explained, pointing out the minute black strings.

Rabbi Friedman then carefully looked at the first piece of unrolled parchment like a crime-scene detective. "Isn't that beautiful?" He pointed to the hand lettering of the Hebrew prayer. "Your grandfather's tefillin are a museum piece."

The insides of the tefillin *were* beautiful, the four individual compartments holding parchment looking like miniature inner chambers in a castle. He resumed his investigation. "This one looks good," he finally declared, finishing with the first parchment.

Whew. If I had to wear tefillin again for the first time since I'd been ordered to each morning at age fourteen, then I was counting on using *this* pair, imagining my grandfather's soul sitting on my head and arms in his old phylacteries, thinking maybe I wasn't such a pagan *shmeckel* after all. Knowing how much he valued these tefillin, and considering I'd never done anything for him during his life.

"Unfortunately," the rabbi said, looking closely at the next parchment, "there's a little bit of water or insect damage on two of the other parchments. These tefillin aren't kosher."

I looked and saw a slight discoloration on the parchment. I was horrified. "Are you sure?"

"Yes. You're going to have to get a new pair. We'll get you the best."

"Look," I said, "what does it really matter if they technically aren't kosher? Doesn't the spirit of what they represent count?"

"No. Then they aren't holy, and no matter how much of a *mitnaggid* your grandfather was, he'd feel terrible if he knew you were davening with unkosher tefillin, even if they'd once been his."

"And kosher," I said.

"I'm sure," he said, looking at the water damage again that had made them *trayf.* "This could have happened last month. In any case, you'll need new ones."

The tefillin were one of the first things that had become valuable to me since deciding to at least try and be a properly silent mensch. And now, because of some technicality, I had to reject them. But the real jive, I was beginning to feel, was not so much the cost of buying new tefillin but the cost of kidding myself into thinking I'd fill the hole in my soul by doing things like wrapping straps and boxes around me.

Still, it actually had felt very nice to be able to see the parchment my grandfather had carried across the world.

"Here," he said, delicately handing me the parchments and horsehair. "If you frame these, they'll make a wonderful remembrance of your *zayda.*"

I took the remnants back from Rabbi Friedman sadly, like a game show contestant reluctantly taking "a lovely parting gift."

He leaned back in his chair and paused. Earlier, I'd taken out my other phylacteries, the ones I'd gotten for my bar mitzvah from my grandfather. Apparently, I'd rendered my own tefillin unkosher by tossing them around heedlessly inside my camp cabin bunk a quarter century before, and Friedman had taken one look at them as if he were staring at something as worthless as a Big Mac.

As I stared at my grandfather's dissected tefillin, the rabbi shook me back to earth. "I'll call Crown Heights tonight and have them next-day air you your new tefillin," he said excitedly.

"Knowing how my grandfather felt, I'll feel sort of like a jerk using Hasidic-made tefillin," I said, hemming and hawing. My anger reboiled—a response he would provoke only a few more times and, it seemed, always on purpose.

I then took a tiny prayer book that would easily fit into my back pocket out of my briefcase and showed it to him. "This is the last thing I have of my grandfather's," I said. "On my bar mitzvah he also gave me this little siddur made in Jerusalem."

"That's great," Rabbi Friedman said. "You can use your *zayda*'s old prayer book when you're putting on your new tefillin."

He paged though the volume, pointing out different passages, looking for the most important prayer in Judaism, the *Sh'ma:* "Hear, O Israel, the Lord our God, the Lord is One." The *Sh'ma* was everywhere, in tefillin, the Torah, the siddur. You kissed the prayer when you touched a mezuzah on the way into or out of a house, and you were supposed to say it as your last words if you were being drawn and quartered by the Inquisition or the SS.

"Is there any *Sh'ma* in particular I should read while putting on tefillin?" I asked.

"Nah," he said, paging to one of many examples in the prayer book, "any *Sh'ma* will do."

"I don't know, I still feel like I'll be betraying him somehow." I felt like I was stabbing an ancestor I actually *knew* in the back, someone who would have died twice if he knew I was chopping apart his tefillin with a Hasid. "I'm a hypocrite," I said, "by thinking it's okay to do that using the excuse that it's in the service of my soul."

"That's okay," Rabbi Friedman said. "First, that's great you're talking about your ancestors. Very healthy. But let's talk hypocrisy. The rebbe once said we would all be healthier as individuals, families, and communities if we took the following concept to heart: 'Jews are not normal.' "

I laughed.

"Wait a minute," he said. "That's not the end. Let's use an example. Say you went into a church, mosque, or ashram and asked everybody if they believed in God and were religious. They'd all say, 'Obviously.' "

"I'm listening."

"But if you then go into a synagogue on Yom Kippur and ask the average Jew who is fasting—until he at least gets home—if he believes in God, you can never get a straight answer. If he's slightly philosophical, he'll say, 'Well, it all depends on what you mean by God.' If he's *very* philosophical, he'll say, 'What am I, a rabbi? I don't *know* if I believe in God.'

"And if you ask that same average Jew in the synagogue on Yom Kippur if he's religious, he'll crack up laughing. He'll assure you he is the *farthest thing* from religious. In fact, he wants to tell you how ultra-assimilated he is. 'Do you know what I had for breakfast?' he wants to tell you."

Now Friedman was on a roll, with a couple of Jackie Mason–like flourishes to emphasize a point. "And then that average Jew in the synagogue on Yom Kippur will invariably say, 'But my grandfather on my mother's side, now *there* was a religious man! But me? Not now. Maybe I was when I was much younger. Maybe I'll be when I'm much older. But certainly not right now.'

"So then you ask the next logical question of that average Jew," Rabbi Friedman continued, no longer using comic voices. " 'If you feel this way, what are you doing here in the synagogue on Yom Kippur?' "

I hadn't gone that year, I silently reminded myself.

"And he looks at you like you're crazy. Even though what that Jew is actually saying is, 'I know today is Yom Kippur, even if I don't have a Jewish calendar. I am in the synagogue, even though I hate the place. I am a Jew even if I'm not religious. God is God, even if I don't believe in Him. And I am here, because God wants a Jew to be in the synagogue on Yom Kippur.' "

"That sure sounds like hypocrisy to me," I countered.

"Well," Rabbi Friedman said, "a lot of us unfortunately *do* dismiss this as sheer hypocrisy. A lot of us say, 'You're not religious, you don't believe in God, so don't come, you're a hypocrite! Why are you coming to the synagogue on Yom Kippur, to show everyone how *Jewish* you are?' "

"I get that," I said.

"The rebbe had a completely different take on this apparent

hypocrisy," Rabbi Friedman said, slipping for one of the few times into referring to the Lubavitch leader in the past tense. "This kind of insanity I've just described is in fact what makes us Jewish, he thought. This is what shows how special our relationship is with God. We are saying, 'He is my God. He gets on my nerves, I don't want to hear about Him, I don't want to talk about Him, but look, He wants me here on Yom Kippur, so that's where I'll be.' "

We stared at each other.

"And . . . ?" I asked, looking for the conclusion.

"And that is *incredible*. That's called *emes*—truth." Lesson over.

"C'mon," he said, "let's have some birthday cake and pizza. It's Muschka's birthday, and she's having a party with her girlfriends."

I was confused. Was this the kind of wisdom I was looking for? Was it worth destroying the very symbols of my family's Yiddishkeit?

Yes. For starters, being tugged by both Judaism and assimilation hadn't worked for me. And every night as I went to sleep, I could still sense the sand falling to the bottom.

Even if I didn't belong to somebody or something, then for the first time in forever at least I felt I belonged a little to myself.

As I was leaving that night, a young Hasidic rabbi named David Greene dropped by to pick up his daughter from Muschka's party and discuss with Rabbi Friedman his work ministering to patients at the Mayo Clinic.

"You from here?" he asked. "I grew up in St. Louis Park."

I was about to answer that I had grown up in Minneapolis and then moved to St. Louis Park myself, when Rabbi Friedman interrupted before I could get the city's name out.

"Nissan's from Karlin," he told Rabbi Greene.

"Karlin? Like Rav Aharon of Karlin?"

"It's near Pinsk," I said, closing the door to go outside.

14

RABBI CARO EXPLAINS
IT ALL FOR YOU

Happy is the man who wears tefillin and fathoms their mystery.
—the kabbalistic book of the Zohar, Chapter 1, verse 129a

The next morning, I called the *sofer* in Brooklyn, the *sofer* who charged $1,000 for a pair of top-of-the-line kosher tefillin. "Yaah?" said the not especially friendly voice that answered the phone.

"Um, I'm a student of Rabbi Manis Friedman's in Minnesota," I mumbled, "and he said I should call you for a pair of new tefillin."

The voice immediately softened. "You're one of Rabbi Friedman's students?" he said. "Hold on."

Momentarily, another voice came on the line. "You're studying with Rabbi Friedman? I'll have a pair sent out express mail, they should be at his house tomorrow. Wear them in good health, *Baruch HaShem!*"

"*Baruch HaShem,*" I mumbled softly back into the phone, but the line was already dead.

"They're here, they're beautiful!" Rabbi Friedman said exuberantly over the phone to me the next afternoon. "How fast can you get over here?"

I've gotten places faster.

After exchanging our usual "How you doing/ *Baruch HaShem*" (he pronounced the question "How you do-ink?"), he hurriedly led me into his study. There, on his desk, in a small black velvet bag, were what I thought were my thousand-dollar tefillin.

I had to admit they were beautiful. The bag was half covered in gold embroidered flowers, six on a branch. Above the petals, the name "Rashi" was inscribed, also in gold, in honor of the unrivaled interpreter of the Torah. I stirred a little laugh out of Rabbi Friedman by reciting the lyrics to a new rap song I'd read about that extolled the virtues of the carrying cases of Jewish religious garments, performed by some New Yorker named Princess. " 'My palms get sweaty and my tongue starts to wag / There's just something 'bout a man with a tallis bag.' "

I guess he thought so too, judging by the excitement with which he handled the bag and its contents. Inside, each tefillin and its attached straps was shielded by a protective black cover that flipped back to reveal the holy box. "He only charged you four hundred dollars," Rabbi Friedman said. "We had a talk."

"Who is the rich man?" I said sarcastically, quoting my Talmud and Oral Law studies of that week. "He who is satisfied with what he has."

Rabbi Friedman handed me the box labeled *"Tefillin shel yod,"* the hand tefillin. "You always put on, and take off, the one for the arm first. As I said, the *tefillin shel rosh* [of the head] are each Jew's crown— the *keter*—and must come off last."

I knew *keter*. According to *Three-Minute Discourses on Kabbalah,* which I'd purchased from a Jewish book club, *keter* was the tenth and last rung to God in heaven from the earth. No wonder the Lubavitch made such a big deal over tefillin—they symbolized part of the final step to God.

Friedman unwound the six-foot black straps of the arm cinch that dangled to the floor. "Don't worry about that," he said. "Okay, put the tefillin on your left arm. If you were left-handed you'd put it on your right."

I was surprised at how quickly the complicated art of tefillin wrapping came back, and I stopped listening to his instructions as out of some primordial consciousness I wound the religious objects the way I'd been taught so many decades before.

The black leather straps, facing out, went around the forearm seven times and then were held momentarily by wrapping them once or twice around the hand. Then the head tefillin went on, the little box worn just above the point of the hairline, with the knot that keeps it in place centered at the base of the skull.

Then it was back to finishing the hand wrap, where from memory I passed the strap between my thumb and forefinger. Instinctively, I then wound it around the middle joint of my middle finger and then twice around the lower joint. When I looked at the wound result, I saw the straps spelling out *"Sha-dai,"* another word for God.

"Pretty good," Rabbi Friedman said, smiling. "Do it again."

So I unwrapped myself and did it again. And again. I felt like Lenny in *Of Mice and Men,* vainly trying to learn not to pet a mouse too hard. Yet after forty-five minutes of intense tutoring, Rabbi Friedman finally had me doing a reasonable facsimile of once again putting on tefillin.

"So you'll do this every morning, yes? Like I said way back, it's the only thing I want you to do every day."

I tried it, religiously, every morning, but didn't exactly feel the power. What was the Ba'al Shem Tov talking about in number eighty-three of his collected tales, when he described the mitzvah of putting on the unwieldy tefillin? The act was so holy, said the founder of Hasidism that, "it can bring man a yearning that will make him want to depart this world. He must therefore bind them with straps, holding body and soul together."

"The heart will follow," Rabbi Friedman promised. "Doing the mitzvah is being moral, and that is an end in itself. You don't need a justification in Judaism to be moral, to be good, to be nice, to be helpful."

"Well *that* sounds like a *Yiddishe hartz,*" I said hopefully.

"Yes it does. But what benefit comes from this morality? That's an immoral question. Say someone comes along and says, 'Can you help me? I really need someone to talk to.' You can either offer your ear, or say, 'If you can't explain to me why we have to talk, then I won't do it.' That last response certainly isn't a Jewish attitude."

He continued, drawing a parallel I didn't see between doing good deeds for others and observing rituals by rote for oneself. "Nor," he went on, "is the position that many people actually have *against* charity a Jewish attitude. Some people say it encourages parasites. 'Let him go out and work,' people say, 'what's his problem?' That's not Jewish. If someone comes along and says, 'I'm hungry, feed me,' you don't say, 'Why are you hungry, and how did you get that way? And where is the money you should have been earning?' First you feed him, then you can talk."

"Well," I said, "how can you compare the Jewish attitude of helping others by trying to become a mensch and putting on tefillin for oneself in the morning? How are they even connected? What is the morality of putting on tefillin, except that it's something we're commanded to do?"

"When we do what God wants," Rabbi Friedman said, "we attribute a significance to Him that shows a deeper humility that only makes us better people. For instance, the first thing we say every morning when putting on tefillin is different from other prayers. We say, 'Thank you, God, for returning my soul, in whatever form You wish.' That does not mean, 'I *love* my life, and am *so* glad to have it back for another day, thank You *so* much.' "

"I don't get it."

"It means that when we pray in the morning with our tefillin, we're not talking about *my* soul. It means, 'I acknowledge that every day my soul sees another day it comes from You.' That is real humility, thanking God for just being alive. It's not for letting you return again as *you* like to think of yourself—as a *macher,* a big shot, self-styled or real, a fancy doctor, a world-famous writer, a *reicher* [rich person].

"And as the body becomes more humble, more diminished than the soul, the healthier we're going to be. Call it Torah, call it Talmud, call it holistic, that's what it is, the connection of mind and body for a higher purpose."

"So what does God get from this?" I asked.

"We don't know what God gets from creation," he answered. "And we won't know unless we're going to study it for many, many years. But knowing what God gets really isn't a relevant piece of information for us. Because, again, being moral needs no justification."

I reminded myself how much I especially believed in his pronouncements when he prefaced them with "I don't know."

"You hear people say, 'All the answers are here, or there, the answers are all inside this.' I say go straight to God and be in touch with your purpose. The purpose, your reason for being, is personal. And when we know which way to go, we are healthy. When we start to forget and lose touch, then life becomes difficult. God needs you to do a mitzvah, be it laying tefillin, giving *tzedakah* [charity], or lending an ear to a troubled soul. Those six hundred and thirteen mitzvoth are your purpose. It has nothing to do with you being forty and suddenly thinking you can be taught the hidden secrets of the universe and what God gets from the equation."

I pondered this. Didn't this make us all the same, robots supposed to follow the same 613 commandments?

"As far as I can tell," I ventured, "we're all doing the exact same mitzvoth. That means we all have the exact same purpose in life. Doesn't that make everybody who tries to do all those mitzvoth, no matter how irrelevant to day-to-day life they seem, kind of like an automaton? Where's the *heart,* the warm Yiddishkeit, that should make us all different, whether we believe in God?"

"No," Friedman said, "because when you do the mitzvah, it's *you* doing the mitzvah. With all your emotions, your past problems, with your family background, with your ignorance, with your knowledge, all of that comes together, that's what makes your mitzvah unique. Every life, every soul, is handpicked. Each person has a mission, a purpose, a function that no one else has. Without that conviction, nothing we say about the meaning of life will have any meaning at all."

I continued placing the tefillin boxes atop my head and wrapping them around my arms when I woke up each morning, then saying the brief prayers Rabbi Friedman had shown me in my grandfather's prayer book. The ritual felt ridiculous at first, then less so.

When I did tell some friends that I was now putting on tefillin, I felt almost ashamed, the way people had looked when they'd confided to me that they were in recovery from cocaine or a gambling addiction.

"Tefillin? *Why?*" they all wanted to know since I'd left the Berlin Wall up against my own community, and virtually all my friends at home remained gentiles. "You're not turning into one of *them,* are you?" my friends continued to ask.

"I like it when I put on my tefillin," I told Rabbi Friedman, "but I don't have any devotion beyond the ritual."

"Whether a person is a schlemiel or a mensch," he said, "a mitzvah is far stronger than them. If they're not well, performing a mitzvah can make them strong."

"Ya know, it's complicated," I said laughing, "all those steps and straps."

"Look," he said, "there is a statement in the Gemara that the sages took a vote on an issue, tallied the results, and decided it would actually be preferable for a person not to be born. Because life is a struggle. So the sages said it would be more convenient if a person didn't come into the world in the first place.

"But now that we are born, the sages said we must, each on our own, struggle to be good. Remember what I said: The foundation of a purpose of life is the absolute conviction that when God creates human beings He doesn't do it in masses."

And then the clincher, the one that Jews I knew used more than any other as the reason they didn't believe in God or Judaism. "This is all very nice," I said, "but if there is a God who chose the Jewish people to serve as teachers to the rest of the world and make humans godly so that heaven and earth could be joined in *tikkun olam,* then how could He have allowed the Holocaust to happen?"

"Because," Rabbi Friedman said, "if God had made a perfect place, then simply put us into it, then it wouldn't be our world, and we wouldn't feel like a part of it. We'd just be cogs in the machine. The reward is that we stop feeling like guests in somebody else's world."

I didn't buy this, but I let it pass.

"I want you to write something for me," he said four meetings later.

"Well, okay, I'll try, I guess," I mumbled, actually quite frightened by the prospect.

"How do you feel about the Fourth Commandment?"

"Honoring your parents?"

He nodded. "I want you to write about it."

"Why?"

"Just an exercise."

He then stood up, walked over to one of his walls of books, and took down a leather-bound volume written in Hebrew. It was one book of the *Shulchan Aruch,* the definitive compilation of Jewish law by Joseph Caro (1488–1575) that explicates everything anybody would ever want to know about the religion and the Torah. Leafing through the pages, he came to Caro's delineation of what the Fourth Commandment really means and began translating it into English.

How, I wondered, does somebody begin showing respect to his parents after spending one's entire adult life not just ignoring them but mocking their values? Meantime, Rabbi Friedman went on with the twenty-four ways Caro had detailed as the path to honoring them, from not sitting in one's father's chair to performing menial tasks for them, from not correcting your parents in public to when it was and wasn't commanded to lend them money. Rabbi Caro even explained how to honor one's folks when one or both have gone insane.

"What about when you've used them for shtick?" I asked.

"Did you mock them?" he volleyed.

"Nothing real. They were just abstractions to the people to whom I told the jokes, nobody knew them."

"People aren't abstractions," Rabbi Friedman said softly, seeming to read my mind. "They're people, created by *HaShem* as individuals. And what kind of jokes can you tell about your parents, anyway?"

"Nothing anybody would take seriously," I said. "The old jokes, literally from vaudeville. I'd say:

"My parents? For the first five years of my life I thought my name was shut up.

"My parents? When I was born, the doctor said, 'What a treasure!' and my folks said, 'Yeah, let's bury it.'

"When I told my parents I was marrying a non-Jew, they both took an overdose of mah-jongg tiles."

"That's it?" he asked.

And I told him of the routine I used to do, about how comically paranoid my father was of anti-Semitism that he interpreted every inconvenience as emanating from a Jew hater. If a movie was sold out or he had to wait for fifteen minutes at a restaurant, I'd joke to people who didn't know him, he'd yell, "Nazi bastards!" Sitting in a dentist waiting room too long? "Nazi bastards!"

Boy, did that shtick get laughs in the old days.

"Is it true?" Rabbi Friedman said.

"No," I said, ashamed. My father never once mentioned the fact that he had virtually no family because of the real Nazi bastards. He was as far as possible from the stereotypical kvetching Jewish mama's boy. Indeed, I told Rabbi Friedman, I'd seen him punch people offering a slur.

"I guess it's my Oral History," I said.

"And how do you honor them?"

"By feeling connected to them and allowing them to feel connected to me. I don't sit in my dad's chair, and I come over and watch football on Sunday. I ask my mother questions about her life, and I go to my grandparents' yahrzeit, even though it's not even required, so I can show my parents I won't forget them when they're gone. I talk Yiddish with my father—how many sons can claim that?" I said cockily.

"Go find out about as much of your background as you can," he said. "*Quote* your parents. Find out about your ancestors. The *more* connected we are to the past, the healthier we become."

"Isn't it a little late for that? All my grandparents are dead, my cousins are scattered."

"It's never too late. You can deal with the past and the future at the same time."

Then he surprised me with a question. "Do you want to have children?" he continued.

"Yes."

"Then start keeping a diary, but put in it only the good things you do. And don't do anything you wouldn't want your grandchildren to read about. Then your descendants will be able to quote *you*."

"But what about right now?" I asked.

"Okay," he said, "another story. A few years ago my mother came to visit from New York. On Shabbos, I was getting ready to say kiddush with my favorite cup. Suddenly she says, 'Why are you using such a small one? In honor of Shabbos, shouldn't you use a bigger kiddush cup?'

"So I used a bigger cup. And Nissan, who's about six at the time, says, 'Pa, that's not your cup!' I said, 'I know, but I'm going to be using it from now on.' He asked why, and I said, 'Because my mother told me.'"

"You're a good son," I said.

"Wait, I'm not done. When I said that, Nissan's mouth fell open. And ever since then, he's been a great kid, I've never had to raise my voice at him. When you connect the generations, everything becomes more true, important, significant, and bigger. Go figure out how to connect your generations."

I went home and began the torturous work of trying to grind words onto paper again. Using my notes from Rabbi Friedman's talk of the *Shulchan Aruch*'s delineation of how to honor your parents, I concocted a couple-thousand-word confection full of jokes and references to how I'd turned my back on them. I wrote it as a humor piece, based on half-truths, generalities, old jokes, made-up facts, and hopefully an insight or two on the parent-child relationship. No harm, no foul, I figured, and since Rabbi Friedman would be the only one reading it I thought he'd enjoy my infotainment account. Knowing Rabbi Friedman's appreciation of how I had to overcome my own self-loathing to fully appreciate my parents.

The point I wanted readers to take away is that no matter what, even if your parents locked you in a closet for years and you loathed them (neither was true), you still had to honor them. I did happen to love my parents, I wanted to make clear, and tossed in an inside joke for my father and Rabbi Friedman's enjoyment: the philosophy of my peasant grandfather handed down to my professional dad, as a reason to honor one's own relationship with the people who made you: "Vat vaz vaz, vat iz iz, and datz dat," meaning parents and their children should move on from any bitter past recriminations or bad vibes and make the commandment work now.

"This is fine," Rabbi Friedman said after he had read the seven pages the next week. "I have this friend who's editor of this California paper *Olam* [*World*]. I think I'll send it to him to see what he thinks. Have you heard of it? It's an insert in papers."

I shook my head. It probably went inside the little newspapers announcing deaths and bar mitzvahs in most Jewish communities in the country. Still, I thought, it was a nice gesture on Rabbi Friedman's part. Perhaps the editors at the unknown newspaper would like my homework for him and ask me to do a piece in the future. I'd have to turn them down, of course: These kind of newsletters never paid anything, and as my spirit healed I planned to revivify my professional career. There would be no time for future freebie articles for publications with names like *Olam*.

"I liked your story," Mrs. Friedman said, entering the study. "At first I thought it was going to be funny, what with all the jokes—and then it wasn't so funny."

I thought nothing of it until I received many weeks later a frantic phone call from an editor at *Olam* who told me she was working on my piece. Among those who'd be joining me in the issue, she said in explanation of why I wouldn't get paid, was everybody from Elie Wiesel to Shmulie "Kosher Sex" Boteach to Michael Jackson.

"*What?*" I exclaimed. "I didn't think that was going to get published!"

"Well, Rabbi Friedman, who contributes often to *Olam*, sent it to the publisher and we're running it. It's long, of course," she said. "We'll have to probably cut it almost in half."

Oh, shit, I thought.

"And where exactly is your paper inserted?" I asked.

"Oh, *The New York Times*, the *Los Angeles Times*, *The Washington Post*, the *Jerusalem Post*, the *Forward* . . ."

Hearing the publications, I almost vomited. My parents would see it. I hung up the phone. She was a very nice woman and a good editor, but by the time she was done with the piece it had lost the point I was trying to make. Still, the read-back she e-mailed me didn't seem incendiary, though I couldn't really figure out how it fit into that issue's topic of "How to Raise Your Parents."

15

SOMETHING TO
BELIEVE IN

*O*lam sent me an early copy of the issue, and I felt knock-kneed and nauseous as I read the headline while standing at my mailbox: "Confessions of a Parent Basher."

I sat down in my apartment and started reading. In the middle of the story came:

For the last several years of my twenties, in the last several years of Manhattan's 1980s, I spent $250 a week I couldn't afford telling a thoughtful, young Yale-trained psychiatrist how much I hated my parents. Or maybe I said I hated my parents but loved them. Or maybe I said I loved my parents, but didn't like them. I can't remember. Like getting cable, seeing a shrink was the fashionable thing to do. After each session, I would imagine being surrounded by thousands of ambitious twenty-somethings, stacked by floors like drones in an ant farm, all telling their thoughtful Yalie psychiatrists how much they hated their fathers and their mothers.

Perhaps Commandment Four had always weighed heavily on me because I knew it was one of the Big Ten I could actually do something about, and also the one I was most likely to violate.

The end of what was published didn't do much to make *any* in our family sound much better.

"*Dad, can you think of any particular times when I've honored or dishonored you?*" *I asked my father one day while I was contemplating this article. We were seated in front of the television watching one of the last football games of the season.*

My father considered my question. "No, I can't particularly think of any times you've dishonored me," he said.

But honored you . . . my father was back to the football game.

"*Aaargh!*" *I said like the cartoon-strip Charlie Brown, lying on his back for the millionth time after Lucy had snatched the ball away just as he was about to kick it.*

And then I remembered.

I knew that, like Charlie Brown lining up the ball for the million-and-first time, no matter what my parents said or how they grumbled, I'd keep on trying.

Today, I even picked up my pen.

The biggest scandal I revealed from the looks of the finished product was that I'd once told someone with a shrink's degree that I hated my parents—even though that had been a decade and a half before, and I certainly felt no need to share that with the world now, especially since I was currently trying to save my future by plugging my past. I hadn't felt the need for his approval for forever, but now I'd slagged him from coast to coast, and all the way to Jerusalem. Amends, not approval, was what I wanted, but how does one even begin after such scandalous, scabrous words, no matter how they'd been changed and taken out of context, the jokes made real by a voice on the phone from Los Angeles?

Within a week, copies began hitting newsstands. The fallout began when my older sister, always my greatest, most outspoken advocate whenever I'd worked myself into a jam, called to find out what had happened. A graduate like me of ten years of Hebrew school who'd majored in Jewish studies at college, taught at an Orthodox day school in Chicago before going to law school, and remained active in the local Jewish community, she listened to my side of the story and quickly assigned blame to Rabbi Friedman.

"You should be angry at Friedman," she said.

And I was. I felt that he should have been watching my back.

"Do Mom and Dad know?" I asked.

"Yeah. You better call."

As I stared at the phone, I was more frightened than I'd ever been after printing a hatchet job on any titan of business or media. They always called afterward, and although I would get reamed by a screaming bully when I returned their calls, my rule had been: You don't dodge the rageaholic rants.

My parents knew, had known about the article for days. I picked up the phone and dialed the first six digits of their number, then hung up. When I finally had the courage to get my father on the phone, he never mentioned the *Olam* article, which he'd gotten that week in his issue of the *Forward* I'd given him as a gift. Until I called him, my punishment was the same as the blessing I'd received from Rabbi Friedman: the meaningfulness of silence.

I felt like the sixth son, the seventh, eighth son, how much room wasn't there at the Seder table? I had become the asshole who not only doesn't show up at the Seder and isn't considered Jewish by his family and community, but is an actively growing *shanda*.

"Hello?" he answered the phone, and I could hear my mother pick up the other extension.

"So you saw the article," I said.

"Yes," he said. "I didn't understand it." I knew he understood just by his tone of voice. I thought of the Yiddish phrase *besser a guter feynt, vi a shlecter freund* (it's better to have a good enemy than a bad friend). Only I substituted the word *zun* for *freund*.

As he listened, I explained that I was just the victim of a bad editing job and that I never thought the words, comic in intent, would hit the light of day. I read parts of the original draft to him, trying to point out the irony and show how I'd really been making fun of myself. In my attempts to break away from my family and suburban shtetl and assimilate, I'd become a carbon copy of hundreds of thousands of twenty-somethings like myself who were doing the exact same thing and telling their shrinks the exact same words. I was just conforming to the rules of a new game, where this time everybody was trying to remake themselves, just like me.

"I got four more copies of your article in the mail today from friends," my father finally said softly into the phone. "One was an insert from the *Forward,* one had been placed for free, I guess, in the *Los Angeles Times,* another from the *Jerusalem Post,* and the other from inside *The New York Times.*"

"I'm sorry," I said in admission of the hideous error I'd committed by first writing the piece, then allowing it to be printed. The article, and what it said, made me feel like a *shanda fur di mishpocha.* It was a serious charge to levy against myself, to admit that you've victimized your kin.

"No," my father said unconvincingly in reply. "You're not a *shanda*; I just don't understand what you were trying to say . . . ," he said, drifting into silence, as I mentally completed the sentence, "at least not any more than you did when you told everyone you were going to be a rabbi, when you married into an anti-Semitic family."

"Thanks, I think I'd die if you thought that," I said for a good-bye, knowing he did think that.

I hung up and closed my eyes as tight as I could, the words with which I'd just branded myself a *shanda* on continuous replay, the first time I'd been tormented this way since the depth of my own three A.M. forever despair.

My next call was to Rabbi Friedman. We'd met a couple-dozen times by now, sometimes when I was summoned to meet him that second. This time, I was going to be the one asking the questions.

I nodded curtly to Mrs. Friedman; the rabbi was waiting for me in his study. Like a prosecuting attorney delivering his opening condemnation, I laid out what the fallout of the article had been. His mellowness remained undented, and my face flushed.

"It will blow over," he promised. "Good will come of you saying how you felt. You didn't say anything disrespectful, you just tried to bring your ancestors and parents closer to you."

"They printed that I hated my parents," I said. "I'm not a prima donna, I'm easy to work with, but they didn't let me know that was how the article was going to come out. Did you?"

"No," he said matter-of-factly. "And anyway, it said that in your twenties you felt that way."

"They turned around the meaning of my article; they betrayed its intended point. They made it sound not about my own self-loathing but about my need to assimilate away from not only my parents' beliefs but also who they were as *people*. Even in my *original* version I was just being hyperbolic, to show *you* I understood the lessons in the broadest terms possible. If I'd known what was going to happen I wouldn't have even written my original draft like that!"

"So you got edited," he said. "You're sounding like a writer again, a real writer who has a pen to put down the truth."

"I've been trying to make changes in my life, including following your advice and connecting to my roots. And now I feel I'm back at square one."

Rabbi Friedman nodded, not exactly chastened but definitely hearing the sound of my new wound. "I've also tried many times to make changes in my own life," he said. "And do you know what the biggest obstacle has been? It's *me*. The stumbling block has been that I can't see myself being better."

I was astonished. I'd never seen a rabbi exhibit such self-reproach before.

"But you're on the road half the year talking to people who want to pay you for your wisdom!" I abjured, but he shook his head. He wasn't self-loathing, I knew that, and Rabbi Friedman was nothing if not a man happy in his own skin. He just, it seemed, had a desire to change things. He was not, he was telling me, infallible.

"It's easy for me to show up somewhere and make a nice speech. Most of the time I don't even know the topic, I find out when I get there. So I make my nice little talk and say that I think having 'family values' is a terrific idea, and of course I can back it up. Yet there are other things I talk about that I don't necessarily believe or practice."

He stared at me. "The point is, I can stand in front of an audience and be very high-minded, but when I get home, I think, Who am I kidding? I want to be more respectable and dignified, but I know I'm just an old goat who doesn't know what he's talking about. You're intimidated by yourself into thinking you can't change—you can't visualize it.

"There's only one way to overcome that inability to change. The moment you decide to change, go home and change something. Move the furniture. Anything. Make some kind of visible change that will help you carry out the resolution you have."

I let out a breath of disappointment. Move the furniture to symbolize the change you know you need to make? What sofa was large enough to push to allow me to make amends to my father and regain my place at the Seder table? "Okay," I said, having no idea what I'd do. "I'll try it."

"Don't worry," he said. "What you are doing are the steps to *kavanah*. Stop thinking of the heavens so much. In the meantime, know that your purpose in life doesn't *have* to involve the cosmos, or be philosophic, or include all mankind. It can be *your* life, as it is."

"My life, like my father and me?"

He held his palms up in his familiar gesture of "It's up to you."

I looked blankly at Rabbi Friedman, like he was somehow supposed to explain how one finds one's own belief. Instead, he leaned back in his chair and explained why he couldn't tell me, even if he wanted to explain his own belief, because he didn't know how. "We come to *kavanah* as individuals, in our own way," he said.

"Let me explain," he went on. "Okay, you know about two of the most famous sages of the Mishnah, Hillel and Shamai, right?"

"Yeah," I said, remembering Hebrew school. "I don't recall too much about Shamai, though."

"That's true. We hear all these stories about the greatness, kindness, and patience of Hillel. And then maybe we hear a story or two about Shamai. Well, maybe you need to better understand Shamai's behavior to understand why I can't help you here, I can't *tell* you a way to faith."

I never tired of his stories.

"Okay, let's start with the most famous story about Hillel. The Gemara tells us that a man came to him and said, 'I want to convert to Judaism, but I need you to tell me the essence of the Torah, the essence of Judaism.' And Hillel said to him, 'What is hateful to you, do not do to others. That's the whole Torah. The rest is commentary. Now go and study.' "

"It's a classic," I said, twisting my lips to pronounce it like Bill Murray's catchphrase.

"But there's another part to that story that happened first," Rabbi Friedman said.

"A prequel."

"Yes. Before the man who wanted to convert went to Hillel, he first went to Shamai, who simply chased him away with a long ruler. Now if we take that story at face value, it sounds like Shamai was inconsiderate, impatient, judgmental, and cruel."

"I knew he was a great scholar, but I didn't know he was such a jerk," I said.

"And yet," he continued, "it's impossible to accept that Shamai, a great sage and saint and tzaddik would be anything less than respectful, considerate, and patient with others. Because in the Mishnah it says those who find favor in the eyes of men also find favor in the eyes of God."

Though Rabbi Shamai's message was right, his delivery was wrong for the unlearned, I thought. No wonder the wanderer had run away. No wonder Rabbi Hillel got all the press.

I don't know if this was the lesson Friedman had planned, but I was choosing my own morals to his stories today. He had been trying to get me to reconnect to my past, my father, all along. He'd made no secret of that. Now he'd told me he too needed to change, that he was his own worst enemy, and that even he was always trying to change the furniture of his life. I chose to take that as a remarkable apology. Even if he had betrayed me, he hadn't meant to, it was for the greater cause of bringing me back to my blood.

And what would a mensch do in response? He would allow Rabbi Friedman, of course, to complete his *t'shuva*.

"Yet there's another little detail to reconsider in the story in the Gemara," he continued, like a Hasidic Sherlock Holmes. I liked this voice too: It was his scholar's slow timbre, and I knew to shut up. It turned out that now Rabbi Friedman was adding a postscript to his story about Hillel and Shamai, once again pointing out, I felt, his own fallibility as he tried to help me find my way home.

"Now it says that Shamai chased the man away with a measuring stick, like a yardstick, in his hand. Why was Shamai holding a yardstick? He was a scholar, a man of learning, not a carpenter. So it must mean that every one of the sages had his own yardstick, meaning that each one had his own measure, degree, and style of service to God. Each saw the Torah in a unique way.

"Shamai couldn't just tell it to him," he continued. "Indeed, he had to chase the man away to find the meaning himself. That's why the man ended up at Hillel's in the first place. Through in this new view of what it says in the Gemara, we don't have a good and bad guy, a good and bad sage, God forbid."

Well, as they say in Minnesota, duh, of course I knew it. There was no Evelyn Wood–speed leap-of-faith course. With age had come laziness, and there was a part of me that just didn't want to accept this fact, to think that after all these hours sitting in this uncomfortable metal chair, I'd have to find my own faith my own self and way.

I couldn't stop thinking about my father. The fact that I'd done a hatchet job on him in print, no matter how unknowingly, had gnawed at me for months, made it impossible for me to think there was any chance of turning toward true *t'shuva,* and I didn't just mean heading in the direction of a mensch. I meant the head-on meaning of *t'shuva* as straight-out repentance. I decided I would make Yom Kippur that year, by myself and half a season too early.

My favorite part of the Jewish liturgy had always been the mass confessional on Yom Kippur, the most anxiety-producing holy day of all when it was determined who would be written in books of Life and Death. True, I hadn't attended those services since God knows when, but I still felt shivers as I remembered everyone in the congregation rising, admitting en masse every sin known to man, beating their chests at each transgression.

So the next morning, after putting on and taking off my tefillin, I donned the tallis my grandfather had given me with my long-destroyed tefillin for my bar mitzvah, and searched out the High Holiday prayer book. I turned to the pages bearing my favorite prayers, said only on this pretend most holy and solemn of holy days. It was the *Al Chete,* Hebrew for "the sin."

Reading the confessions in Hebrew, I beat my chest with increasing velocity until the skin over my heart literally hurt. "We abuse, we betray, we are cruel," I read, pausing after each sin to bring my clenched fist against my chest. "We destroy, we embitter, we falsify. We gossip, we hate, we insult. We jeer, we kill, we lie. We mock, we neglect, we oppress. We quarrel, we rebel, we steal. We are unkind, we are violent, we are wicked. We are xenophobic, we yield to evil, we are zealots for bad causes."

And on and on and on. At the end of each stanza of admissions, standing alone in my room, I would sing the mournful refrain I'd never forgotten: *V'al ko-lam El-ohai slichot, slach lanu, mi-chal lanu, kap-per lanu* (For all these sins, forgiving God, forgive us, pardon us, grant us atonement).

Though the God part still meant sort of nothing to me, or wasn't the brass ring, tears were streaming down my face by the third sentence of the prayers. So many of the sins in my case seemed true.

I'm sorry.

It wasn't belief, I knew, it was nostalgia for when I didn't have to try and beat the feeling into myself. Like the most *kavanah*-filled believers on the actual Yom Kippur, I was praying to *feel* the electricity of the prayers, the way I'd once done, when the old words just naturally shot through me.

The next morning, looking back at what had happened, it began. It felt like a pounding in my temples, like the beginning rush of an LSD trip before it's kicked in. I didn't know what it was at the time—maybe a headache.

16

CONNECTING

*Honor thy father and mother in order that thy days may be
long upon the land that the Lord thy God giveth thee.*

—Commandment Four

The one thing that my father and I had always agreed about was
my grandfather's wine. The brew was so righteously tasty, he'd
won the honor of making it for synagogue religious sacraments in the
village. The wine that accompanied each *"l'chaim!"* and clinking of
glasses in the shtetl came from my family's generations-old secret recipe.

Now, I simply wanted to show my father one thing before time ran
out on either of us. After all our years and my egregious screwups, I
needed to share something Jewish with him, or there would be nothing Jewish between us, which meant, I realized from Rabbi Friedman,
there really would be *nothing*. It had to be the two of us working together, not just saying prayers, and we had to sweat.

I called my father.

"Vos macht a Yid?" I asked cheerily.

"Fine," he said.

I got right to the point, no shticking. "Can we make *Zayda's* wine
this year? I'd like to learn how to do it."

"Really?" he said. *"Really?"*

I shuddered, feeling instinctively he'd heard my plea to return. Maybe Rabbi Friedman hadn't been a schmuck getting me in such hot water with that article. Perhaps he knew he had to push me away from himself and toward my real father, my real roots.

Still, though the fallout had been bad within the family, the act had now kicked me toward an attempt to perform true *t'shuva,* repentance, that went beyond breaking bagels on Sunday mornings. Now my father, for the first time, was considering letting me take part in a holy family ritual that had been discarded because of lack of interest.

"You know it's a secret recipe, it's made just *so,*" my father reminded me. "There's just been no one in the family who wanted it."

"I can keep a secret," I said.

"I've gotta get back to work," he said. "I'll call you from home to discuss this. If we do make it, we're going to do it like we always did it, the hard way, like Pa did, like I did it with Pa."

"And when I was little I used to do it with you and your pa," I pointed out.

"I seem to remember you watching," he said. "But, wise guy, do you think you could do it yourself, you know the secret recipe, you even know how to operate the wine press he schlepped from Europe?"

"Well, no," I admitted.

"You know what it means that he schlepped it from Europe? That he risked his life for it? He could hide his tefillin in his pocket, but this was something you couldn't conceal."

"Yeah, I've got an idea."

"Think about whether you're up to it. I don't want to order those hundreds of pounds of grapes," he said, not meanly but as a matter of fact, "and have you not show up so I have to do it all alone."

"You won't be alone," I promised.

"One question before I hang up," he said. "Why do you suddenly care about making *Zayda's* religious wine?"

"C'mon," I responded, "it wasn't always about religion. I know where a lot of that wine went. You once told me that he never sold it, even in Prohibition, but he, uh, *shared* it outside the shul, right?" Though I knew it wasn't true, I liked wishfully to think at least a little bit of an outlaw hiding out in his Orthodox trappings, like Meyer Lansky or Bugsy Siegel, tough Jews I'd long respected far more than religious ones.

"Listen to you," he said. "Your grandfather was very *frum* [pious]."

"Hey," I said, half perturbed, half laughing, "I'm *frummer* than you are. When's the last time *you* put on tefillin?" I asked, preparing to give him the *zotz* (needle).

"A couple months. You?"

"Twenty minutes ago," I said truthfully.

"You're kidding."

He paused. "You sure you want to make the shtetl wine this year?" he asked a third time. "If you really mean it, we don't have much time to prepare. I'll have to order Concord grapes—I hope the farm I used to order them from is still around, it's in Michigan."

In the old days, when three generations of my family were involved in making the wine, my *zayda* was the general, my father his lieutenant, and I was eventually promoted from curious kid onlooker to *shtarker* (heavy lifter). Back then it had felt like an honor to be involved in the backbreaking labor behind the delicate chemistry my grandfather was whipping up that he'd been famous for a lifetime ago in Karlin. Even as an old man, the artisan of the vine continued spending whatever time he had left perfecting and experimenting, via his tongue and a test barrel set apart from the year's annual batch.

He was a tough son of a bitch. The only time I'd seen him cry was when I was a teenage pallbearer lowering his wife's simple plain box, as per Orthodox tradition, into the ground after a fifty-five-year arranged marriage. It was the kind of marriage set up far more stringently than the mere introduction I'd been offered not so long before in the Los Angeles shul.

Even as she went into the ground, my grandfather didn't offer a tear but rather a wail that seemed to come from another century and species. The only time I ever heard such a lamentation from the soul was from my father, who to this day I've never seen cry. No, once, when he emitted the same howl standing over my just-dead grandfather's grave.

My grandfather, as per tradition, would always take the first sip from his kiddush cup filled to the brim with his concoction, after he did the blessing over the wine, when he led the huge Seders I attended as a child. My grandmother, sitting directly next to him, waited patiently as the cup made the rounds the other way.

She was used to delays; she'd had to wait seven years to join her husband who'd also left behind his two daughters, my two Russian aunts. Aaron Karlen would send for them to join him in New York as soon as he raised steerage fare. But World War I broke out and emigration halted, things happened that no one ever asked about, and when my grandfather was finally able to send the fare, it was seven years later from someplace called Minnesota.

He simply refused to talk about the old world or his own father, my great-grandfather Rabbi Zussman of Karlin, whose name I deciphered from the Hebrew on my grandfather's grave. Nor did anyone have any idea who my grandfather's grandfather was. Yet even after my grandfather died, my father and I kept making the old wine for a few falls until I graduated high school. Yet making the old-country wine hadn't even come up as a subject for decades.

But now, led without a word by Rabbi Friedman to honor what you could find from your past while there was time, I told my father I wanted back in. And no longer, I told him, did I want to do just the mindless *shtarker* work. I wanted to know the *secret*. It had been handed down in our family from generation to generation, until it stopped due to the indifference of my brother, sister, and me.

"Why now?" he asked again.

I gave up on you a long time ago, I thought I heard.

"I want to make the wine for old time's sake," I replied. "I mean old *man's* sake."

"Hey," the late-septuagenarian said, "I'm not that old. I could still take *you* out."

"Not you. Another old man. *Your* pa."

"Zint es iz oyfgekumken dos shtarben, Iz men nit zikher mitn lebn" (Since dying became fashionable, living isn't safe). My father laughed before hanging up, his way of saying, "Okay, but you don't remember what you're getting into."

Five days later, I was back at my usual spot at Rabbi Friedman's house, excitedly telling him how I'd continued busying myself trying to bury my ghosts and honor my ancestors, even the ones I'd never heard of, long dead, naturally or via pogrom. I left out my apostasy in doing a portion of the Yom Kippur service several months early, by myself. "Somehow," I said, "all this, connecting with my past, making a public effort not to debase myself as a Jew, makes me feel like I'm doing a mitzvah."

Then, astonishingly, he said, "Every mitzvah we do involves rejoining a little piece of that Divine spark of God—that spark that was *separated* from God, at Creation. Each mitzvah brings back the peace, reunites a portion of the *Shkeinah,* the part of God that's *in* Creation, and *HaKodesh Borachu,* the part of God that's *above* Creation. Though this sounds mystical, it's actually close to our actual lives."

"How?" I said, realizing we were dancing around *tikkun olam,* the healing of the world by uniting God's female aspect (the *Shkeinah*), which watches humanity from the temporal world, and God's masculine aspect, which views humanity from heaven (*HaKodesh Borachu*). The two mates, say Hasidic sages, were blown apart when the world was created in the process known as *tzimtzum.* This *tzimtzum* separated *Ein Sof* (without end; the mystical books' most esteemed name for God) from Himself.

With that breakage was born a finite Creation by separating heaven and earth, the first sentence of the Torah. Now the universe existed, but until the tear was mended, there would be no healing. And how would that be done? Through performing mitzvoth, said Rabbi Friedman.

"All of us were created to perfect the world," he said, "to create heaven on earth, to bridge the distance that separates heaven from earth."

When that happened, the male and female aspects of God would join in surprisingly sexually charged imagery in the Kabbalah, achieving the *tikkun olam* that had become necessary when the universe was separated at birth from the harsh reality of earthly life, and the beauty of what might be in *O'lam Ha'bah*.

17

WELCOMING THE QUEEN:
THE MIRACLE
OF THE SABBATH

*Sabbath is the anticipation of the messianic time, just as the
messianic period is called the time of "continuous Sabbath."*

—Erich Fromm, the social psychologist from a
rabbinic family who renewed his interest in
Judaism after a lifetime of atheism

*K*avanah never officially arrived. What did come after my last recent talk was the realization that I believed that putting on my
tefillin meant something more than binding myself in black leather
straps. The feeling, it seemed, had sneaked into my apartment without
my knowing it and into the black boxes.

I didn't make a Kierkegaardian leap of faith, roll on the floor and
begin speaking in tongues, or phone Rabbi Friedman and tell him I
wanted to be immediately fitted with a Hasidic fedora and tzitzit.
Rather, after putting on my tefillin and finishing the brief prayers
one morning, I just felt as if I were actually looking forward to the
coming day. It was the first time I'd felt that way since I'd been
thrown into the abyss of my own despair.

I went to a drawer where I'd stored the remnants of what may or may not have been my grandfather's century-old pair of tefillin, rubbed the soft bag, and said, "Hey, *Zayda,* I think I get it. A little."

I put on James Brown, yowling along with him until it struck me that this felt like the first time I'd danced in two decades.

No, I didn't feel like I was touching God, but god damn it, at least I wanted to dance and hear the beauty of music again! I called Rabbi Friedman to tell him the news, in slightly different words. He sounded pleased but not exactly surprised. "What are you doing for Shabbos?" he asked. "Why don't you come over here?"

I'd been dodging their invitations for months. He didn't have to tell me that his invitation implied that I was meant not to drive, write, move a blade of grass, turn on a light, make a phone call, or even carry a watch.

"Homina-homina-homina," I mumbled inwardly, like Jackie Gleason.

"I haven't been *shomer Shabbos* since I was a teenager," I told him, invoking the words that technically mean "guardian of the Sabbath" but in reality denote one who cuts himself off completely from the world for the seventh day, as per the Ten Commandments. In Exodus, the importance of the Shabbos has been interpreted by some sages as encompassing the entire essence of Judaism:

> Remember the Sabbath day, to keep it holy. Six days you shall labor, and do all your work; and the seventh day is the Sabbath of the Lord your God. You shall not do any work; you, nor your son, nor your daughter, your manservant, nor your maidservant, nor your stranger within your gates. For in six days the Lord made heaven, the earth, the sea, and all that is in them; therefore the Lord blessed the seventh day and made it holy.

Putting on tefillin every morning by myself and going to Rabbi Friedman's house to talk once a week was one thing. But to be locked up with his family, no matter how nice they were, from sundown on

Friday to twilight's end on Saturday, seemed unbearable. I imagined Friday night and interminable Shabbos morning services, with enough other prayer meetings to equal the sum total of hours I'd spent in a shul in years.

The importance of keeping Shabbos was impressed even upon the Jewish slaves of Egypt, Rabbi Friedman had taught me only that week. "Moses told Pharaoh to give the Jews a day off to rest. Of course, Pharaoh didn't care about Shabbos, but Moses was able to convince him that with one day off—say, Saturday—the Jews would be more efficient at building his pyramids."

Now there was a pause on the phone. "Come for Shabbos," he said again calmly.

"Why?"

"Because maybe things are beginning to kick in."

"With all due respect, Rabbi, I don't want it to 'kick in' the way it kicked in for you."

"I understand," he said patiently. "But 'kicking in' may also mean understanding simply that God needs you to fulfill the mitzvah of keeping Shabbos."

I felt honored. Still, I was feeling drawn into a trap. I had plans that weekend to go see a Lou Reed show and have two very unkosher dinners with friends. Now I'd be stuck doing . . . I wasn't sure what. I thought back to the Friday night dinners of my youth, which I knew were still a version of the same dinner being served at thousands of tables in my own Jewish suburb.

"Okay," I said, feeling completely pinned down yet simultaneously honored.

"But you better hurry," he said. "You've only got thirty minutes until sundown."

I got to the Friedmans' with seconds to spare. Like my first visit, I was happy to be invited while irrationally semihoping they'd forgotten, or that no one was there. Mrs. Friedman was already preparing to light the Sabbath candles, one for each child.

At summer camp, at home, *anywhere,* these ceremonies had always been an occasion for back-of-the-room mockery. Now the candle lighting just looked beautiful.

The Sabbath, kabbalistically, was always portrayed as a female who oversaw the earth and was the spiritual equal of the masculine God in heaven. And these opening prayers over candles were meant, as was said in a constant refrain of *L'cha D'odi* sung every Friday from Hasidic to Reform households, to "welcome the Sabbath queen."

Shabbos wasn't a rabbi's holiday. It was one symbolized by a woman, the *Shkeinah,* benevolently overseeing a world trying to perfect itself. So when I arrived at the Friedmans', the rabbi's wife lit the Shabbos candles, and then we headed off to shul.

As the entire synagogue belted out *L'cha D'odi,* I felt hands on my shoulders, and for the second time that day I was dancing, this time in a circle of grabby men who'd nabbed me to gavotte around the room with them. They looked on the verge of tears of happiness as they gleefully sang verse after verse of the song, each followed by a refrain of *"L'cha Doe-di li-rot kalah, pi-nay Shabbat Ni-Kablah"* (Come, my beloved, to meet the bride; let us welcome the Shabbat).

I usually hated this kind of behavior, couldn't stand being pushed and pulled against my will into a group, no matter what they were doing, but especially dancing. I hated being a junior counselor forced to jump up on tables and sing joyfully in Hebrew for no reason at all. I'd always refused to give in to what seemed like planned spontaneousness.

Yet this felt real, and I wasn't embarrassed after my initial shock wore off. Even if I'd been ashamed, I realized, no one could see me.

Behind a screen, separated from the men, were the women. It was this screen that had chased so many women away from all Judaism, labeling it as the traditional symbol of a sexist, misogynistic religion. I'd heard what I thought were all the stories and excuses for one or another, starting with how putting men and women together would distract both sexes from their prayers. I would have to ask Rabbi

Friedman about this during the traditional time of Sabbath reading and reflection.

Dinner lasted for hours, as Chana and Chaya oversaw the distribution of a grand spread that began with the usual gefilte fish, chicken soup, and herring and then rounded the globe of Jewish cooking. All the dishes, of course, had been prepared before sundown and were now simmering on heating elements that wouldn't be turned off until the end of Shabbos tomorrow. Jokes and riddles mingled with conversation among the dozen people seated at the long table.

Though as usual I still often had no idea what was going on, I didn't assume the role of village idiot. I asked questions when I knew what to ask but otherwise just tried to relax into the warming glow of a family celebrating. I pounded fist to table to the *nigguns,* tried to figure out why they all seemed so happy and at peace. Meantime, the rest of the world seemed gone.

Over and over, Rabbi Friedman would close his eyes, begin banging on the table with his fist, and boisterously start singing more *nigguns.* I knew from my own reading of the writings of the Rebbe Aaron of Karlin that these weren't just nonsense melodies but kabbalistic hymns that were the keys "to higher spheres and sanctuaries." The *nigguns* would sometimes go on for a minute, the plates on the table rattling with the fists pounding out every beat, and suddenly peter out into a story.

He started his tale. "A very bright young man was once sitting next to the previous rebbe at dinner, and he said, 'Sitting in jail for Yiddishkeit is a mitzvah. And sitting twice is even a higher mitzvah, beyond the letter of the law. But *five* times, Rebbe? I don't know, isn't that a little bit of *arrogance?*' "

I laughed. I then tried to sound smart, to not just be an onlooker but a participant in the conversation. "I always liked how my father wouldn't talk about Jewish gangsters going to jail; he said *'heder'* instead. I thought that was a great euphemism: using the word for 'school' instead of 'prison.' "

Unfortunately, as the words came out and I saw the table's nonre-action, I felt like a dope.

Still, Rabbi Friedman focused on me like a meaningful contributor to the conversation, not a dunce, even as he corrected me. "Heder *does* mean school, but literally it means 'sit.' It makes sense that American Jewish criminals called prison 'heder.' In Russia too, 'sitting' meant jail time. The previous rebbe was arrested and 'sat' five times, once when he was only twelve. It was a badge of honor. Four of our five rebbes have been in prison." (Only Rebbe Schneerson, the last one, didn't serve a term.)

"Still," I ventured, "it must have been hard to know the penalty for simply being found out as a practicing Jew."

"Actually," Rabbi Friedman said, "in America it's much harder, not because you can be whatever you want to be but because you can do whatever you want to do. This is much harder. People in America don't realize you can't change *who* you are.

"In the shtetl," he continued, "if Tevye the milkman strutted to the front of the synagogue wearing a fancy fur hat, everyone would look, laugh, and say, 'Who does he think he is?' In America, they'd say, 'Tevye has a new fur hat, he must be a new person!' "

Everyone nodded their heads, including me.

Soon the dishes were cleared and grace was sung. I fell into a deep sleep in one of the rooms used when the house was full with the rabbi's fourteen children and their families.

By the time I was fully awake, I was in my suit, back in the syna-gogue a couple of blocks away, and the synagogue *shamus* (sexton) was asking me if I wanted an aliyah—to publicly bless the Torah before one of the seven portions that would be chanted that day. I nodded okay and hoped that I wouldn't stumble over the Hebrew words to the prayer that I'd sung hundreds of times.

As I heard myself being summoned to the Torah by my Hebrew name, identifying me by my parents' monikers and tribe as "Nissan ben Mordechai vu Chaya Ha' Levi," and began shaking with sweat.

I walked up to the podium, looked down at the Torah, and from ancient sense memory took the end of my tallis, kissed it, and placed the tip of my prayer shawl atop the spot in the scroll where the reader pointed, then looked at the laminated sheet in front of me printed in Hebrew.

I then did something I'd never done before but had heard my father do hundreds of times when he read Hebrew. Before World War II, European Jews pronounced a particular letter with an *s*—*saf.* Yet when Israel and modern Hebrew were invented, the new state was eager to wipe out memories of the Eastern European ghettos and the weak, Yiddish-speaking Jews who allowed themselves to be slaughtered. The old-world Hebrew letter pronounced *saf* was changed and now pronounced *"taf,"* with a hard *t.*

It was an epiphany.

Emes became *emet*—the truth that could animate a golem to life. Only the Hasidim, and some stubborn Orthodox Jews from my father's generation, pronounced the letter with an *s* sound. I certainly never had. Yet as I chanted the prayer, I suddenly was using the old-fashioned pronunciation that my grandfather had used and that my father refused to give up when saying prayers.

"Barchu es adonai ham-vorach," I sang, as opposed to the *"Barchu et adonai . . ."* I'd always said before.

Back at the Friedmans' house after services, I felt a variety of conflicting emotions. I remained elated by the adrenaline rush of successfully chanting an aliyah before such a tough and demanding crowd. I liked the nondescript little synagogue, without decoration, and the smell of sweat of men and women in deep, beseeching prayer.

Yet it wasn't really men *and* women, it was women sitting *behind* men. Were my mother or sister, more saintly than I'd ever been, or any of my female friends, less worthy of a spot near God's Torah?

I brought up to the rabbi the need for the Hasidim and the Orthodox to separate men and women during prayers. I didn't really care about the screen itself; if I someday actually joined a synagogue, it wouldn't be Orthodox, so it wouldn't even be an issue.

Yet if Rabbi Friedman gave me what I deemed a sexist explanation, wouldn't that cast a shadow over other things he said as well? He took me into his study. I guess he sensed my problem, for he sidestepped the question of the screen and went immediately to the differences between men and women.

He didn't go back to the answers I'd always heard from Conservative and Reform sources: Men were thought by the Orthodox to be so weak that they needed to be protected from the sight of a woman's leg while praying. Yet now Friedman seemed to be saying men were just plain and simply *weak*.

"These days," he began, "a lot of us think men are from Venus and women are from Mars. But the Torah says something quite different. Man was created from dust, which really is the same as saying that men were created out of nothing, because dust does not create people. God said let us make man, so man was made out of nothing. And that which comes from nothing always carries a deep-seated awareness of its own nothingness.

"The male psyche, the male ego, lives in fear of its own nonexistence. That's what tortures and haunts the male psyche, it's the demon he carries around. Even if we as men have achieved, does that mean *I* am now something, or is my achievement itself insignificant and nothing, like the dust I was created from?"

"I hear you," I said. "I have twenty years' worth of clippings at home, and plaques and trophies and books . . . and for years I've felt like nothing."

"Exactly. And usually men try to cover it up, or deny it to ourselves, or overcompensate and become aggressive and arrogant to hide our feelings of insignificance and nothingness. A man's greatest fear is annihilation. Men are mortified that they can be revealed, discovered to be nothing, reduced back to zero, feeling they've never amounted to anything. So the male psyche, which needs to go from zero to ten, is terrified of discovering at the end, when the dust settles, that he never got past zero and that he's still a zero."

"Fine," I said. "So that's why men can't stop trying to achieve. But what about women?"

"Women didn't come from nothing. The Torah says they came from humanity."

Uh-oh, here it comes.

"That's not a negative," he said. "Women don't have this male problem of fearing annihilation because, not coming from nothing, there was never a moment in the existence of the female psyche where she experienced herself as a nonbeing, as a nonentity.

"She never has to be afraid of being a zero. Treat a woman like she's nothing, and you don't annihilate her. On the contrary, she becomes morally indignant because there's an injustice here. So what threatens a man most is annihilation; what threatens a woman most is injustice. And that's why the Talmud says that a man should honor his wife more than himself because a woman is sensitive to injustice. A woman's tears are always felt in heaven."

"Isn't that putting women on a pedestal you said the Gemara prohibited?" I asked.

"Not at all. Today, as we come closer to the healing of the world, now men have to shift to the more feminine mode of knowing that there is something precious, good, and holy in the universe that doesn't need to be achieved or acquired. We have to learn how to go from one to ten, a very feminine thing, not zero to ten."

Thinking again about the screen separating men from women in highly observant synagogues, I remembered a trip I'd taken to Los Angeles a couple months before. Rabbi Friedman had given me the name of a part-Hasidic, part-Orthodox synagogue in the Fairfax district, where I was staying, that was run by one Rabbi Lisben, an excellent and friendly rabbi who'd become Hasidic after surviving the

Holocaust. I'd gone to his shul several times, mostly out of loneliness.

I'd been impressed with how helpful the men were to me as I tried to follow along in the prayer book, and how, at least here, men and women were separated by a screen that was laid out side by side. Instead of putting the men in front of the women, the setup was separate but equal. Between services, the screen would be taken down, and the men could see the women only yards away. As I glanced about the synagogue, one of the men who'd helped me follow the service several times quietly said, "Are you married?"

"Divorced."

"Umm. We have many connections here, you know. Look over there, isn't she beautiful?"

I looked across the room at a woman who looked to be in her midtwenties. She was dark, a Persian, and indeed one of the most beautiful women I'd ever seen. She was staring back at me, but in a way that seemed to suggest someone had told her to look my way so I could look her over. I felt immediately embarrassed *for* her, like she was a horse whose teeth I was supposed to inspect. Meantime, my own pride roared, like I needed anybody's help in such matters.

"Yes," I said to the man, "she's quite lovely."

"She comes from an excellent family," he said, by which I thought he might mean rich. "Very religious. How long you in town for?"

"A couple weeks."

"Maybe we can arrange an introduction. Come to shul every morning for a little while. Do you have tefillin?"

"Yes."

"Well, come, and let's see what kind of Jew you are," he said.

Though he probably meant well, I immediately felt insulted, embarrassed. I was still too afraid, I realized, of even the *notion* of being in an actual Jewish community, to commit to a Jewish woman, family, or environment.

"Los Angeles is an excellent simulation of real life," Rabbi Friedman had said. Maybe, I hoped, afraid I'd cut off my nose to spite my face, this woman was an excellent simulation of a way to be invited into the Jewish community.

"Me?" I asked. "You want to know what kind of Jew *I* am? How do I know what kind of Jew *you* are?"

He backed off, and away, and I never went back to that shul. I'd felt a flush of shame as I realized he'd only been trying to do a genuine mitzvah for a stranger.

And now, on Shabbos in Rabbi Friedman's study, I realized I had indeed felt my male psyche wounded. He nodded. It *was* as if I were in fear of being reduced to a zero, a loser who needed strangers to find him potentially suitable mates or he might spend the rest of his life alone . . . or back in the land of *Jew him down.*

"You aren't ready," he said. "You're still on the rebound."

"When it comes to women, I like to make my own trouble," I told Rabbi Friedman with both pride and shame, "and I guess I always have."

As I told Rabbi Friedman the story of my experience in the L.A. shul, he said nothing but simply kept stroking his beard.

"Oh, well," I mumbled. "As my grandfather used to say, 'Vat vaz vaz, vat iz iz, and datz dat.' "

He still said nothing.

"At least I'm still quoting my ancestors, that's some kind of miracle, isn't it?"

He still said nothing and stared at me.

I looked out the window; the shadows of dusk were beginning to fall. In minutes, Shabbos would be over. "Wait a minute," I said. "I think maybe I *have* been experiencing a miracle."

"How so?"

"Well, I always thought miracles as meaning having the oceans split, or God coming to talk to you. But maybe it can be simpler. This is the first weekend in decades I haven't looked at a clock. I didn't turn on a light. I didn't have or want a nickel in my pocket. I sang *nigguns*. I danced around a synagogue and didn't feel like an idiot. I went to bed at ten-thirty. I don't even remember worrying. I was *shomer Shabbos*. That's *some* kind of miracle, isn't it?"

"Yes, it is," Rabbi Friedman said, smiling broadly, slapping my knee, and getting up. "Come on, miracle man," he said, indicating it was time for the short home service symbolizing the end of Shabbos, "let's go do *Havdalah*."

18

BOOTLEGGING THE SHTETL WINE

Over the bottle many a friend is found.

—Yiddish proverb

The red Concord grapes came from the Michigan farm several weeks later via a truck that dropped four hundred pounds of fruit divided into twenty-pound "lugs," or boxes, in the driveway of my parents' home.

"Let me get the press," my father said. But remembering what Rabbi Friedman had read to me from Joseph Caro's *Shulchan Aruch* about doing menial labor for your parents, I stopped him by putting my hand against his chest and went into the garage. There, leaning against the bike I'd used in seventh grade, was the century-old contraption that looked like the Tin Man's head in *The Wizard of Oz*.

We worked like stevedores. We set the old press atop a forty-gallon barrel; as my father loaded the fruit into the hopper, I turned the crank with the desperation of someone trying to raise a child who had fallen into a well. We didn't say a word as we worked, but I couldn't help but marvel that we were *working together*.

Only one family member in each generation, my father said, was taught the precise combination that yielded the wine. Now, because of the war, we were at the end of the line for the wine. It was sacramental enough in spirit and body to please the village rabbi yet still carried the wallop of a Joe Frazier uppercut.

Prohibition? Not for my grandfather. He'd received a religious exemption to keep making his wine for the synagogue. And if the leftovers went to the neighbors, so what? It wasn't like in New York, where Irishmen posing as rabbis were selling Jewish sacramental wine. My grandfather's jack, after all, was free.

By the 1930s, his mason jars were going out as Christmas presents to neighbors named Olson, Swenson, and Anderson. Always willing to provide a free ecumenical snort to the good Lutherans of Minneapolis, my grandfather died, as Willy Loman would have had it, "well liked."

As we began work, I asked my father to tell the few stories he knew about his father. The tales were about a heroic peasant who survived as an old man who'd never fully recovered from a white-hot poker shoved up his crotch by the shtetl "fixer" who'd failed my grandfather as a young man in trying to make him unusable for the czar's army, forcing my grandfather to flee for the new world.

Now, to me, making the wine and hearing the few old stories seemed as important as my reading the Torah, tutoring kids for their bar mitzvahs, and arguing with rabbis over the finer points of Talmud during my senior year in high school or college.

After those days were done, I was gone. But here I was, cranking the press.

After the four hundred pounds of grapes were crushed that day, we poured in about eighty pounds of sugar and covered the barrel. "So what's the secret?" I asked my father. "I know you can't write it down, but can you tell me?"

"It's not something you can say," he said. "It's something you have to taste, to *feel*."

Exhausted by our exertions, he lay down on the grass with his hands behind his head, and I plopped down next to him.

The wine sat, and every five days or so, I drove to my parents' house, and we uncovered the barrel, reached down, and stirred it with a two-by-four wood plank. Each visit, my father gave me a little plastic cup to take a taste just so I could gauge what seemed to me the infinitesimal changes in fermentation. "That's not something you normally do too often," he said. "That's just so you'll know."

We funneled out the dregs and spread them on my parents' garden. A crowd of birds descended on the muck, and in minutes the yard was filled with drunken sparrows. "This is going to make a great story," I ventured, watching the scene that looked like a cross between Hitchcock's *The Birds* and Bukowski's *Barfly*. I wasn't thinking of stories as in articles, but as tales to begin passing down to, God willing, hoped-for descendants.

I myself had so few stories about my ancestors, and it bothered me.

So I'd try again with my father. "Did you ever think of becoming a rabbi?" I asked.

"I was going to be," he said. "When I was sixteen and graduating high school and Bet HaMidrash [the last two years of higher learning at Talmud Torch for exceptional students], my teacher Albert Gordis advised me to prepare to become a doctor, not a rabbi. He said if I became a rabbi I'd go crazy with synagogue politics."

My *zayda's* job had been to get his immediate family out of Russia, the only one of all the relatives to escape; it had been my father's job, I figured, to reconnect the rabbinical line.

My father grew up in a monolingual American home, and his Yiddish was so perfect people would have thought he grew up in the old country with the *alter-kackers*.

He would have thrived as a rabbi, just as he was still thriving at seventy-eight as a full-time primary-care physician. Still, he hadn't done it, and considering the shame and familial disconnection my same decision had caused, I couldn't understand why he'd never mentioned it to me.

"How did your father feel when you told him?" I asked.

He ignored my question, instead reminding me of the pictures in the family scrapbook of himself with a tallis over his army uniform, blowing the shofar as he led High Holiday services for the Jews aboard the troopship taking them to Asia for the invasion of Japan, which Hiroshima made unnecessary. He added many other examples over the years, in different venues, when he'd had to step in and play the rabbi-without-portfolio.

As if he were an easygoing attorney offering mitigating circumstances to a jury, he reminisced how he had stayed religious enough to have kosher meat shipped to him and his bride when he was doing his internship at the Mayo Clinic in the still mostly goyish desert of Rochester, Minnesota. "Did you ever go out with a non-Jew?" I ventured.

"Once," he said, and I was shocked. "She was a nurse when I was in my residency in Chicago, before I met your mother."

"Was it serious?"

"I guess so. We once took the train to Green Bay to watch the Bears play the Packers."

"What happened?"

"I couldn't break your grandfather's heart," he said.

"Like you broke mine," he didn't have to add. We sat for a few minutes, saying nothing.

"Did you ever almost leave Minneapolis?" I then asked.

"Once," he said. He was twenty-two and in the army in Japan right after World War II. Shortly before his tour ended, he received a great job offer in in Yokohama. He weighed the idea, then decided to take it. He sent a telegram to his parents in Minneapolis, telling them that their only son wouldn't be back after all.

A three-word Western Union response rocketed back from Minnesota: "COME HOME BUM."

Knowing the answer, I asked, "So what did you do?"

"I came home," my father said, without a trace of regret.

All the sparrows eventually sobered up and flew away, and six weeks later the wine was ready. I'd learned the secret at several steps along the way: this much stirring, that much waiting.

On one of my visits before the batch was done, I wandered into the garage and took a close peek at the wine press. Turning it this way and that, upside down and sideways, I saw in barely readable bas relief the words "Lee Bread Crumber Patent June 1895 Antrim, New Hampshire."

"Um, Dad," I said, "come look at this. I don't think this wine press is from Russia."

My father came over and looked at what I'd found. "Holy shit, you're right."

He looked over the manual machine and realized what it was. "This is a crumber, not a wine press. People would put bread loaves in here and grind them into big crumbs. This isn't a wine press at all."

He paused.

We stared at each other and started laughing. Soon, we were howling so loudly that we were lying back down on the ground holding our sides. "I guess that story about the wine press," my father said, giggling, "was just a *story*. So much for legends."

"Not so fast," I said. "Maybe he brought his wine press from Russia and discarded it when he got to America. If he got tired of schlepping it around, maybe he got rid of it and just got some local machinery to grind up the grapes."

My father and I were still laughing, trying to stifle ourselves, but our laughter came out now like gales of wind. "If . . . ," he said *"mein bubbe vot gehat batzim, vot zi geven mein zayde."* (And if my grandmother had balls, she'd be my grandfather.)

There was no bolt of lightning.

But oh, my God, I thought, I *believed*! Just as the Ba'al Shem Tov had said, God could be in a blade of grass—or a bread crumber from the nineteenth century and Antrim, New Hampshire.

My grandfather had remade himself with his American grape crusher in his own way. It was the act, not the artifact, that was important to him.

Now, *that* seemed like a *Yiddishe hartz*. Lying on the ground, I was joyously laughing with my father.

A quarter century after my grandfather had died, I can see him both as a youth on the run and an ancient man leaning over the wine barrel, stirring what was inside with a two-by-four. If only I could talk to one, or both, of those men he'd once been.

I knew I came from a people who have a tradition, but for the first time in two decades it didn't seem so ridiculous to actually *keep* some of those traditions. That feeling seemed like a true bridge between Rabbi Friedman's Hasidism, my grandfather's Orthodoxy, my father's uber-Conservatism, and my own long-term assimilation.

Something had sneaked up on me as I made my grandfather's wine my grandfather's way. I'd begun to trust my gut again. It was my bus ticket back to my Judaism. What was left, I knew, was to connect with the future.

19

THE MISSING JIGSAW PIECE

*Rabbi Shimon says: There are three crowns: the crown of
Torah, the crown of priesthood, and the crown of royalty, but
the crown of a good name is superimposed on them all.*
—the Talmud's *Pirke Avot* (Ethics of Our Fathers), 4:17

When I came upon Rabbi Shimon's statement about the importance of a *shem tov*—a good name—it conked me like
the comic strip Mrs. Katzenjammer's rolling pin. I'd reclaimed my
Jewish pride from the lost and found, but more important, I'd discovered within myself the feeling of having reclaimed my good name *from*
my former self-loathing self.

I no longer felt like the opposite of a *shem tov*—a *shanda*. A *shanda
fur di goyim*, a *shanda fur di shtetl* or *fur di mishpocha*. Most of all, I no
longer felt as I did when I'd first come to see Rabbi Friedman, a
shanda fur mir—a scandal to my own soul.

I could at last live within my own skin.

I'd come across Rabbi Shimon's statement while reading at home
one Shabbos a month after making my grandfather's wine.

As Rabbi Friedman had shown me at his house, Shabbos was an
excellent time to dip into any book of the Talmud—to contemplate

and come up with my own conclusions, as long as they were *Jewish* solutions. So I would crawl through each sentence of the Torah portion during the week, which usually took an hour or two; on Shabbos I began sampling other ancient works like *Pirke Avot,* part of what was once the Oral Law of the Torah.

Meanwhile, Rabbi Friedman's demands upon me, besides staying in touch, were few and undemanding. Was I wearing tefillin? Was I *shomer Shabbos?* Did I read the week's *parsha?* Those were his only questions.

In fact, he never even asked those questions. We never talked about the week's Torah portion, unless I wanted to. In time, the most intriguing character in the Torah to me was no longer Cain or Abel, but Moses.

In the old days, he would have been a worthy target of shtick: *"So Moses is on Mount Sinai, and he says, 'This would be a great place to build a hospital!' "*

No more. I had found the "Divine spark of light" that the Ba'al Shem Tov had said was in every living thing, down to every blade of grass, every singer that made me tap my toe, every joke that made me laugh with joy.

True, I still hadn't yet found a Jewish community in which I felt comfortable. And I still fell prey to occasional bouts of longing for something *else* Jewish. This gnawing was nothing like the despair of disconnection from everything I'd once loved and believed in that had brought me originally to Rabbi Friedman's door. Rather, it was the feeling of incompleteness that comes when you lock together all the segments of a difficult jigsaw puzzle but maddeningly can't find the last piece to complete the picture, even after you've looked under every piece of furniture in the room.

Maybe, I figured, I'd come far enough—that this longing *was* the missing piece that had kept Jews forever looking for the right answer. At the very least, after all, I once again felt wired into Torah and, just as important, into Yiddishkeit—the folk wisdom, customs, and habits that formed the core of my Jewish identity, self, values, and pride.

Still, as Rabbi Friedman had said, one ultimately has to go back to the Torah for answers to the most vexing questions, because "it is kind of a how-to manual for life."

For me, that meant going back to mulling the riddle of Moses one more time. Here, after all, was a man who had uncomplainingly transcribed the details of his own death while God dictated the Torah to him on Mt. Sinai. Who never got to the Promised Land but saw it in the distance from a mountain—talk about not finding the last piece of the jigsaw puzzle. I couldn't forget how he named his son Ger, "stranger," in the same *parsha* where the words "stranger in a strange land" appeared.

Okay, I wasn't looking on from a mountain at holy territory I knew I'd never reach, but I'd been a stranger in my own land, to my tribe, and to my own father. Most of my inability to see what kind of Jews my father and I were had been solved, but the point of my journey, I realized, wasn't to find out if I had been missed by my father when I came back. Rather, it was about whether or not I was still going to be as vulnerable as I had been to his measurement of me as a fit Jew, and vice versa.

I didn't have to come back to my father to come back to Judaism, though that we'd found each other and given each other a break was gravy. If the *Olam* debacle had taught me anything, it was that I indeed had to honor him.

I liked and loved the guy, I realized, and even if I hadn't, as Rabbi Friedman had said when we first met after my father finished making the wine, "Honoring one's parents is not the same as loving one's parents. Love is a whole different subject. It has its own purpose and need and place in the heart. Honoring is a completely separate topic. To bring food to the table, to carry the bags, to go out and run an errand, all the menial tasks that your parents would need to do for themselves, you do for them. In that way you honor them. That's the literal definition of honoring parents."

"But how can you separate that from loving them?" I'd asked.

"Like I said, whether you love them at the time, or ever, is a separate subject. And that's why God can have in the Ten Commandments, without any exceptions, that you honor your mother and father. It doesn't matter what you think of them, how wise or good they are, or how strong and helpful they've been to you. Honoring can stand on its own."

I nodded.

"If you do that," he continued, "then the love that may not be there at the moment will eventually find its way back. Even at the worst moments, when the relationship is in the dumps, we can honor our parents, and by doing that we honor ourselves—and prepare ourselves for a healthy future."

Still I remained plagued occasionally that something was missing. And even though I knew that this feeling of a fugitive peace hiding from me somewhere meant my journey back to Judaism wasn't over, though I wasn't sure why, I began seeing less and less of Rabbi Friedman. He could help me locate it, but I sensed that this part of the trail I'd have to navigate largely on my own.

It was partly by choice, as I tried to jump-start my life while still laying tefillin with all my heart and trying to understand the Torah portion. I began trying to earn a living again, doing the only thing I knew how—subsuming myself in some foreign subculture, trying to understand it in a way that I'd never tried to understand my own Judaism for all those decades.

I'd always loved disappearing into those other worlds, forever calling my job, "running away to join the circus."

Now, even though I'd found that the answer was not in someone else's subculture but my own, I had to hit the road again, even if that meant missing my weekly meetings with Rabbi Friedman. My first major excursion was to cover the Sturgis, South Dakota, motorcycle rally, when five hundred thousand riders converge on a tiny Black Hills town for ten days of carousing, camping, and worshipping at the altar of Harley-Davidson. Some were true Hell's Angels outlaws; others, endodontists playing *Easy Rider.*

The noise of motors on Main Street in Sturgis was beyond deafening, the characters and color a feature writer's dream. Yet it became immediately apparent to me that this now just felt like a job. Willfully losing myself in alien territory for the excitement of being a stranger in a strange land, a *ger,* just didn't excite me anymore. Not that I could stop—I had to make a living. But I was going to make a living as *me,* a connected Jew.

The second morning of the motorcycle rally, I climbed out of my sleeping bag at the Buffalo Chip Campgrounds outside of town, the most notorious of the tent cities at the event. I had to stay at the Buffalo Chip for proper "color."

After all, that was where Sturgis's infamous nightly breast-baring contest was held. There, women who referred to themselves as "Harley bitches" exposed themselves onstage, accompanied by hundreds of motorcycle outlaws yelling the traditional call of "Show us your tits!"

In another time I would have gone to the contest in order to capture a paragraph or two of sexy color—what would a motorcycle rally be without sexy color? But remembering Rabbi Friedman's Shabbos teachings, translations, and interpretations from *Pirke Avot* about what it means to treat women with respect, I instead went to a staid concert in town. Even just observing someone else's exploitation, even if I could rationalize that I was just getting the facts, seemed a violation of what a mensch would do.

When I woke up each morning at the Buffalo Chip, I took out my tefillin and siddur from my backpack. I suppose I could have put them on and quickly prayed inside my tent, but I remembered Rabbi Friedman's admonition that one of the reasons tefillin were so important was that they could be worn outside for all to see, to show you weren't afraid to say, "I am a Jew."

So I did it, and the motorcyclists cooking breakfast around me gawked and elbowed each other with amusement. No one said a word—to my neighbors around their tents, I was obviously a bigger freak than any of them proudly proclaimed they themselves were.

Rabbi Friedman continued his grueling travel schedule, spending half his life crisscrossing the world in the role of the Hasid everybody liked. Sometimes he'd lecture with combative Orthodox rabbis in Johannesburg, then four days later to large secular crowds in New York not on what Madonna or Mick Jagger said, the answers to life mysteries weren't found in bite-sized morsels of easily digestible Kabbalah; then on to Buenos Aires, to give his familiar talk to assimilated Sephardic Jews on why they should stop torturing themselves about finding the perfect mate and just get married and start having children.

His absences didn't bother me; it was always a schlep to St. Paul anyway, and the long weekly evenings, surrounded by a culture from the eighteenth century, ultimately began to exhaust me. Sometimes Rabbi Friedman would call me four or five times before I'd call back. I didn't mean to be rude, I was just afraid of being asked to come over and do Shabbos his way, when I now wanted to do it mine, which often meant doing it all alone. We would still get together, but not every week, maybe every month.

A year and a half after we'd first met, another of his rabbi sons was marrying the daughter of a prominent Los Angeles Hasidic rabbi, and I was invited to go out to the coast for the joining of the two grand clans. I debated with myself for weeks on whether to go—it is considered the highest compliment Hasidic parents can receive to have someone dance at their son's or daughter's wedding.

But I had to get my own life going, and I had an assignment and due date from New York that week. And anyway, I still didn't have any money. To make sure they wouldn't or couldn't offer to pay my way with charitable tzedakah, I faxed the Friedmans my regrets. I explained why and also reassured them that I was still *shomer Shabbos,* laying tefillin, and reading my *parshot.* I also always wrote down a Yiddish idiom in its Hebrew script to show I was still on the bus.

The phrase I used in declining the invitation to their son's wedding meant "you can't be in two places at once," but this time it made sense.

The literal translation was a little different: *Mit ein tuchus, nit ken tantzen arois geven tzwei chosseneh* (With one ass, you can't dance at two weddings).

Two weeks after he returned, I sat next to Rabbi Friedman in his office at the same stations where we'd met perhaps thirty times. Catching up with small talk, I finally told him of my nagging sense that I was still missing a lesson.

"I see," he said, and we sat there wordlessly, him drumming his fingers on his desk, me looking around the room. I thought of the first time I'd come here and how I'd been thrown by the mere sight of the mezuzah hanging on his doorframe, which held the *Sh'ma*.

After that long-ago afternoon, I'd take my tiny prayer book from my bedside table. This siddur was the one made in Israel that my grandfather had given me on my bar mitzvah, and I'd say the *Sh'ma*, just as Rabbi Friedman had instructed me.

And now, the prayer ran through my mind again: *Shma Yisroel Adonai Elohainu Adonai Echad* (Hear, O Israel, the Lord our God, the Lord is One). Monotheism 101.

The *Sh'ma*, the most important prayer in all Judaism, said countless times each day in prayer by the devout; yelled defiantly before martyrdom as the embers of Torquemada's Inquisition began to crackle; mumbled, sobbed, or shrieked by scores of naked Jews, some my relatives, whom the Nazis had stripped on their Anschluss through Russia, the blood of my blood spilling into unmarked graves.

The *Sh'ma,* in times perilous or quiet, handwritten inside the mezuzot on the doorposts of anybody who identified himself as a Jew. As Rabbi Friedman looked on wordlessly, the rest of the prayer ran through my head by heart, until I suddenly stopped at "and these words which command thee this day, teach them to unto [the] children . . ."

Bingo. The missing jigsaw piece.

I had connected to my Jewish past and present, but I now realized what I had to do was pass it forward. Not necessarily Rabbi Friedman's Judaism, or my father's, or that of the St. Louis Park Jews whom I'd so often condemned and ridiculed in the past. I had to pass on, I felt in my gut, *my* Judaism, which in truth was just a quilt, with patterns supplied by all of the above.

I'd loved teaching those scores of kids for their bar mitzvahs when I was growing up. Even now, the most fun in my life was working low-paying adjunct teaching jobs, or no-paying mentoring gigs at inner-city junior highs or my suburban high school. But tutoring a child for his or her bar or bat mitzvah—that's where I'd see what kind of Jew I'd become and what kind of Judaism I preached, maybe even the type of rabbi I'd have been.

True, my practical skills were rusty, to put it mildly, in the art of chanting Torah. And the cantillation of the haftarah—a passage from the Prophets sung after the Torah—and all the synagogue prayers and blessings had all but faded from my memory. I would just have to figure it out all over again. I was confident of my ability to pass on my notions of Yiddishkeit. Yet even if I went off on folk-wisdom tangents, priority one would have to be a hard-core understanding of the ancient skills I'd long forgotten.

Now the problem was to find a child. It had to be the right kid. And as such, my motives were not entirely altruistic. As Hasidic Master Rabbi Yitzchak Meier of Ger said, "Being a teacher is a worthwhile endeavor. That way you may learn a few things yourself." Especially, I figured, with the right kind of kid.

I cleared my throat.

"Have you thought of the lesson you missed?" Rabbi Friedman asked.

"Maybe I need to *give* lessons," I ventured. "Maybe I'll tutor a child for his bar mitzvah? You know, see if I can get the barnacles off my *mapachs* and *pash-tas*," I said, referring to two of the ancient notes used to chant the Torah.

I came back on my usual Thursday the next week. It was fall, and unlike when I'd first shown up on the Friedmans' doorstep, my body had
resumed its sense of itself. I again could feel the difference between
hot and cold. Once again we took our usual positions in his study: he
behind his gray metal desk, me in the industrial-looking chair to his
side whose grooves, I now imagined, I'd worn in and burnished, *tuchus
offen tisch,* literally with "my ass on the table," in usage, having "gotten
down to brass tacks."

"First," I said, "I want to thank you."

"For what?"

"For teaching me how to always answer a question with a question," I said, and we both laughed.

He nodded and smiled in acknowledgment.

"Second, I want to ask your advice. On teaching."

I'd started asking around among friends if they knew anybody
whose child was going to have a bar or bat mitzvah in the next six to
nine months.

Ever since I was a teenager, I'd tried to make whatever class, tuto-
rial, or seminar I was teaching so much fun that the students couldn't
help but show up with their hearts and minds, willing to work hard
for the show.

Bar mitzvah lessons had been hideously boring when I was growing up, just as they had been at the turn of the century for Jewish im-
migrant children, and just as they had been, I imagined, in biblical
times. In the early twentieth century, Irving Howe reported in his classic *World of Our Fathers* that a Hebrew teacher was typically "an un-
happy *melamed* [unordained teacher] . . . usually an elderly man who
feared and despised everything he found in the new world, [so] he
turned to the teaching of children, whom he often also feared and despised."

At best, the *melameds,* who always called themselves "rabbi," Howe
went on, "were earnest, medieval men, zealously trying to impart un-

wished for knowledge to unwilling youngsters . . . always on the alert for the mischief the young devils might invent and with a stick in hand for admonitory persuasion."

Not me. I liked to encourage my students to be young devils, to cook up mischief, just as I'd tried to do as a pupil. Just think it out smartly, I'd tell them, show up, make your trouble, and see if I could either handle your questions, blow or return your volleys or not, or come to agree with you.

Wrote Howe, "Thousands of pupils would remember the *melamed* with a cordial hatred, though later, some historians would judge him to have been as much a victim of circumstances as were his victims."

Not me. Just as Rabbi Friedman was the Hasid everybody liked, I'd always tried to be the Hebrew or college teacher, or high school mentor who not only wasn't a dipshit but was fun. Someone you could even *talk* to.

But did Rabbi Friedman have any tips for me to add to my rusty repertoire for a bar mitzvah student, if I could find one?

I wasn't surprised that his initial response, after a healthy pause punctuated by his usual beard stroking, was based in Torah. "If you want to talk about improving a child's education, then we have to talk about improving life itself. If we want our children to be better people, *we* have to become better people. If we want children to absorb and internalize good things, then we have to *surround* them with those good things. That is the best lesson."

This I thought I could do. I now sensed that I knew the important things that could make one, or at least me, feel connected to Judaism. I hoped I could surround a student with those notions without smothering his own divine spark of curiosity.

A teacher of a child, Rabbi Friedman said, must not act on impulse. "That's just a reaction, and the child feels he doesn't have to take that seriously. But when the teacher's message is not a reaction to what is happening at the moment, but part of a thoughtful process, it has two benefits. Number one, the child knows that you are taking him seriously because you have been thinking about his lesson even when the child was away. He actually is quite smart and aware, and knows if this lesson is something you've prepared, mulled over, that you truly wish to say, and it's not a momentary, instinctive reaction to an event. Then the child knows you're taking him and the subject seriously, and that causes the child to take it seriously as well."

"So it's just showing that you care," I said, nodding my head like *I* was the *chochem* (wise man).

"It's more than that. It's the *compliment* the child feels knowing you were preparing to tell him something even while he wasn't there. That you take his development, growth, and education quite seriously; that you give it thought on your own; that you prepare a lesson; that you determine, you choose, you decide what the proper next lesson is, what the child needs to hear now, what needs to be corrected at this stage, at this point."

"Is it okay that I like to let them have fun?" I asked. "To fool around while they're learning? I've found they learn *better* if you let them fool around." I paused, thinking, *Like* we *had fun.*

Rabbi Friedman pursed his lips and told me exactly what I wanted to hear. "To teach in a healthy fashion, you must include some way of encouraging a child to be a child. You know, we keep telling children how to be adults. We keep preparing them for adulthood. We send them to school, we tell them, because when they grow up they're going to need to know this and know that. We get them degrees because when they get a job they're gonna need to have those degrees."

"So?"

"So most teachers are always talking about what they need to be successful adults. We have to tell them how to be successful children first."

20

ONE PAGE AHEAD
OF THE STUDENT

*The question is not who is learning . . . the question is—who
is teaching?*
> —Rabbi Adin Steinsalz, the most famous Jewish
> scholar of the twentieth century for his epic
> translation and commentary of the entire Talmud

"You're hired," Lu Lippold said. "You're not going to screw
up my daughter's bat mitzvah, are you?"

"I promise I won't," I told her, hiding my nervousness.

"Okay. Come next Shabbos and have dinner with me, Bruce, Mira,
and Ellie."

I gulped. I'd have to drive over to their house, which meant I
wouldn't be *shomer Shabbos* that week. The only reason you could
break the rules was in a matter of life and death. Yet because this was
what I sensed might somehow prove to be the final piece of my jigsaw
puzzle, I thought this case fit into the allowable dispensation excuses. It
took me two seconds to decide not to ask Lu if we could get together
Thursday instead. This was *my* Judaism after all, I remembered, not
Rabbi Friedman's, or my father's.

"You sound nervous," Lu said.

"Nah. I've successfully tutored a hundred bar or bat mitzvah kids out of a hundred," I said, sounding a little, I thought, like a late-night TV pitchman. "Not one kid blew it, or even froze."

"And when was the last time you tutored someone?"

"Nineteen seventy-seven."

"Wonderful." She laughed. Thank God I knew Lu slightly, and her husband, Bruce Johnson, a recent convert to Judaism. They were my kind of Jews: funny, smart, urban, progressive, and more into the mitzvah than the bar. They belonged to an inner-city shul, Shir Tikvah, of liberal bent yet traditional practice.

Lu added that her daughter would be expected to chant her Torah and haftarah readings, as well as the Sabbath service's entire liturgy, in Hebrew. I was glad to hear that Mira had been studying Hebrew for years.

"No sweat, Lu," I had said as nonchalantly as I could, knowing full well I'd be one page ahead of my student.

That Friday, I pulled up to the Lippold-Johnsons' two-story house in southwest Minneapolis, feeling only a twinge of guilt for breaking Shabbos by driving through the city. I was mildly surprised to see a mezuzah hanging from the doorpost. This was going to be a Reform bat mitzvah, after all, and though I knew the movement had tightened up a bit—for God's sake, kids were now reading Torah!—I still remembered the way Reform Judaism had been practiced during my youth.

No one wore yarmulkes or tallises in the Reform synagogues of the Twin Cities back then, except my father, who didn't mind standing out like a sore Jew when he had to go to a family function or a friend's kid's bar or bat mitzvah at a Reform shul. He was as much a *mitnaggid* against the Reform as against the Hasidim.

Over the years, Shir Tikvah's membership had swelled to several hundred families, and its founding rabbi, Stacy Offner, became known in the Jewish community as an inspiring, sometimes intimidating figure. She was a one-woman Ellis Island for displaced, intelligent, or searching Jews, beginning an outreach program to fifth sons and daughters banished from Seder tables all over the city, the intermarried and cast out, and the curious who would attend synagogue only if they could pray in jeans and sandals.

Now their crowd was a mix of professors, gays, freelance intellectuals, wealthy nonconformers, liberal Democrats, scattered African Americans, and many, many socially progressive families, both nuclear and divorced.

Lu opened the door, behind which stood Elianna, their Gidget-cute sixteen-year-old with freckles, braces, and a blond ponytail. Inside, I noticed a full shelf of Hebrew and Jewish texts stretching for six feet above and behind the dinner table. Something smelled great in the kitchen. I'd seen more than my share of sterile suburban Jewish houses, and this place glowed *haimishe*—a warm, Jewish home.

Lastly, completely hidden behind a huge, honking tenor sax, came all five foot two, ninety-five pounds of Mira (Mé-ra) Lippold-Johnson, would-be bat mitzvah, wearing an impish grin astoundingly similar to Nissan Friedman's. "Hey," I said, sticking out my hand.

"Hey what?" she said, slapping it, her smile turning not quite evil but definitely mischievous. Perfect. I wasn't surprised to learn she'd been the only female to try out for her school's tackle football team.

Lu and I went into the kitchen to see her husband, Bruce, standing over a kettle of pasta. "Come, *bubbelah,* have some vine," the suave, Lu said in a mock old-world Jewish mother's voice.

"So you ready?" she asked.

"Feed me and I'm yours."

"Great. A guy who just rediscovered he's a Jew after twenty years away decides he wants to experiment in time travel by tutoring my daughter Miranda for her bat mitzvah . . ."

She raised her voice toward Mira in the living room "WHICH IS ONLY HALF A YEAR AWAY AND SHE HASN'T STARTED STUDYING THOUGH ALL HER FRIENDS HAVE!"

After dinner, which replicated the Friedmans' right down to the last matzo ball, Mira and I sat across from each other and I laid out her options. "Okay," I said, "there are two different ways of going about this, the easy way, and the hard but more fun way. The easy way is just to memorize your Torah and haftarah portion, and the prayers, like they're just songs on the radio. That will take a month. We can get one of those tapes they churn out and sell for each week's readings, I can come back in June, we'll hard-core it for a month, and you'll have it memorized so you can spit it back out the day of your bat mitzvah, and forget it all forever by the start of your bat mitzvah party."

"We're going bowling," Mira said. "My folks are going to cook."

Thank God. This all was going to end with kids being kids, and not a grandiose, grotesque *Goodbye, Columbus* scene of chopped liver swan excess.

"They already gave us those tapes. That's what my friends did. They just memorized everything," she said. "Terry pretended she was read-ing along, but she really just held the *yod* [Torah pointer] on the first word of her portion the entire time she was singing."

"Then there's the hard way," I went on. "That's the way you learn how to actually read the Torah and haftarah, learn the couple dozen mu-sical trope and their note combinations, and how to apply them to the words in the Torah. That way you'll be a *real* Torah and haftarah reader, and can chant any portion you want during the year. It's a pain in the ass to learn, but it's worth it. If you want the honor, you'll always get a big gig on any Shabbos or holiday if you actually know how to read.

"And if you want the hard way," I added, "the lessons also involve learning Yiddishkeit, different aspects of truly being a Jew."

"Yiddishkeit?" Mira asked.

I took out the 1965 *Encyclopedia of the Jewish Religion.*" 'Yiddishkeit,' " I read. " 'The Jewish way of life as expressed in the practices of the tradi-tional Jewish religion and its customs. The term has a warm ring for the Jew, denoting the positive aspects of Jewish habits, often of folk origin.' "

"What's that mean?" Mira asked.

"Everything that's not biblical in origin," I said. "In other words, nothing which you'll have to do on your bat mitzvah. But it's just as important if you want to be a mensch."

"Huh?"

"If you want, we'll just study Yiddishkeit a few minutes at the beginning of every lesson," I said. "You know, topics like Jewish jokes, goofy Yiddish terms, Jewish heroes, folktales, how to tell nice Jewish boys from bad Jewish boys—that stuff doesn't change, not really, whether it's from three thousand years ago or yesterday. But it's all Yiddishkeit and has as much to do with Judaism as what you'll be doing on your bat mitzvah."

"Yeah," she said, giving me a sidelong smirk that I understood to mean, *You better not be boring.*

"First," she said, "I don't want to just memorize my portions and prayers."

"Okay," I said with mixed emotions, knowing I'd now for sure have to learn everything flawlessly too.

"And Yiddishkeit. I want to try that."

"Okay."

Now I was even more scared. In the old days, parents pretty much worried about the bat mitzvah party and left the Torah reading and Yiddishkeit to me. But Bruce and Lu seemed to have read every book of the Bible, the Talmud, and all the commentaries, and wanted to talk about it. I wasn't sure I could win a game of "Stump the Tutor."

"Thou shalt not worry the parents by making them think you're a dope," I remembered and fretted.

"So we'll feed you dinner every time you come over, okay?" Lu asked.

"I'd feel like a total *shnorrer*," I said. "Hey, Mira, here's your first lesson in Yiddishkeit: You know what a *shnorrer* is?"

"What?"

"It's a professional beggar; but more than that it's a beggar who believes he's naturally entitled to anything anybody else has. He's the one who walks into your house, opens your refrigerator without asking, sees eight kinds of pop, and says, 'What, you don't have *regular* Coke?' "

"I know people like that."

"Okay. This is the end of lesson one: the *shnorrer*'s obnoxious sense of entitlement, old-country version. This takes place in the shtetl. Every week, this one *shnorrer* gets five kopecks of tzedakah from the local business *macher*—that's a big shot." I interrupted myself. "You know *tzedakah,* Mira?"

"Charity. And whoever gets it isn't supposed to know where it came from."

"Excellent. It's one of the most important things in Judaism."

"Finish the story," Mira said.

"Okay. One week, though, the businessman had nothing for the *shnorrer,* let alone his usual five kopecks.

" 'I'm sorry,' he tells the *shnorrer,* 'it was a bad week.' "

" 'You have a bad week,' the *shnorrer* says, 'so I should suffer?' "

Everyone haw-hawed, and I looked at my watch. "Okay, we have time for Yiddishkeit lesson number two, but next week we get serious about learning some Torah. Anyway, you know how you can describe all of Jewish history in one sentence?"

It was an old joke, but I saw only shrugs. "They tried to kill us; we won; let's eat."

Time to get serious, "Now, schedules. How about this. We'll begin by meeting once a week, build up to twice a week, and then three right before the big day. You don't want to learn it too fast; you'll get bored and be flat for your bat mitzvah, and bore *us.*"

I drove home un–*shomer Shabbos* but feeling joyous with the idea that at least I'd found the puzzle piece. Squeezing it into the jigsaw, of course, would not be as easy.

———————

I arrived the next Thursday with a briefcase stuffed with lesson plans and audiovisual aids for Mira.

When I sat down with the twelve-year-old, I asked, "So did they give you any specific outline of what you'll need to know?"

"Yep." She handed over several Xeroxed sheets. I looked in horror at some of the requirements for a bar or bat mitzvah at Shir Tikvah:

> —A minimum of five years of Hebrew studies at Shir Tik-vah . . .
> —Leading the congregation on Friday evening and/or Saturday morning in the following prayers: Barchu, Sh'ma, V'a havta, Avot, Gevurot, the Torah service prayers, and Kiddush . . .

I gulped. I was perhaps two-for-seven on these prayers I used to know by heart.

> —Chant the Torah blessings and 15–25 verses of Torah . . .
> —Chant the Haftarah Blessings and 12–21 verses of Haftarah . . .

Alongside these four requirements, someone had drawn an arrow and the notation "June"—when Mira was supposed to have all that done. A similar arrow clumped together some of the next requirements:

> —Prepare a translation of your Torah portion, in your own words . . .
> —Prepare a D'var Torah. This is a 2–3 page double-spaced typed "sermonette." It is an opportunity to talk about your thoughts on the Torah portion, the Haftarah portion, the Bar/Bat Mitzvah experience, and the people who helped you get to this special moment . . .

"I wrote a haiku for my *d'var Torah* on my bar mitzvah," I said, hiding my own fear behind shtick. "I still remember it."

Today I am a man
Tomorrow
Seventh grade

"You did not," Mira said.

I smiled—she was right. "Check this out," I continued, handing over a slim volume called *Haiku for Jews* from which I'd taken my faux *d'var Torah.* I felt like Rabbi Friedman handing over one of his volumes for perusal at our first meeting. "See if you find anything interesting."

"This is funny," she said.

The last item on the Shir Tikvah bat mitzvah agenda was:

—Attend services at Shir Tikvah at least once a month in the
    year prior to your Bar/Bat Mitzvah. Check in with the
    Rabbi after each service to record your presence on the
    Shabbat Attendance card.

"Whoa," I said. " 'Check in with the Rabbi'? 'Shabbat Attendance card'? Sounds like you've got a control freak for a rabbi."

Mira shrugged.

I then turned the page and saw some of the specific instructions for the teachers:

GUIDELINES FOR BAR/BAT MITZVAH TUTORS

Begin working on the blessings. . . . Follow soon with the Torah portion. This material represents the bulk of their participation. If you are able, teaching the trope is the first priority. . . .

I [the rabbi] will meet with each Bar/Bat Mitzvah candidate

about six weeks before the service to hear his/her progress. . . . In the last six weeks, focus should be on fine-tuning the Hebrew portions, writing the English translation of the Torah portion, the summary of the Haftarah portion, and the D'var Torah. . . . By this time they should know everything that they will be doing in the service.

"My God," I said, "she *is* a control freak. There's not one mention here of teaching you Yiddishkeit."

"Oh, great," said Mom Lu from the kitchen, "the tutor is going to be at war with the rabbi."

"Screw this schedule. We'll spend the whole time learning everything at our own pace. Like I said, if you learn your Torah and haftarah two months early you'll be as flat as Wile E. Coyote after he's fallen off a cliff chasing Road Runner."

I crumpled the sheet of requirements into a ball and threw it over my shoulder. "No problem," I said, though some of these requirements definitely were going to be. "This stuff will be a snap, and we'll have plenty of time to study Yiddishkeit," I said, careful to reach behind me and decrinkle the page and put it in one of my folders.

"Can we start with Yiddishkeit?" Mira asked.

"You know Groucho Marx?"

"He's funny."

"Well, he once tried to join the Beverly Hills Country Club, which he thought he could get into because he was famous, even though they didn't allow Jews in at the time. They turned him down, and you know what he said?"

Mira shook her head.

" 'My daughter is only half Jewish. Can she go in the pool up to her waist?' "

Mira laughed.

"Okay," I said, taking out my old Tikkun for the first time in front of her. "Enough Yiddishkeit. Let's check out this Torah portion."

Actually learning how to read the Torah or haftarah, as opposed to just memorizing one portion, is as painstakingly repetitive as the single day lived over, over, over, and over in Bill Murray's comedy *Groundhog Day.* Learning the all-important Torah portion meant going over, over, over, and over the same eighteen assigned sentences of the weekly portion, *Ki'Tetze,* from *D'varim,* the last of the five books of Moses, a volume better known as Deuteronomy of the Pentateuch.

I warned Mira about the endless banality of learning how to read the Torah by quoting the Talmud, changing two words to the feminine: "[S]he who repeats what [s]he has learned one hundred times cannot be compared to one who repeats it a hundred and one times," I said.

"I thought I wasn't going to *memorize* things but *learn* them," Mira said.

"Oh, you will, I promise. Actually learning the notes is going to mean going over everything *three* hundred and one times. Now, at any time if you get too bored, and you decide you want to memorize everything, just say the word, and like I said I'll come back in June and this nightmare will be over in a few weeks."

She laughed and I smiled, but I was halfway hoping she'd wimp out and take the easy way out, allowing me to follow her.

I went to Rabbi Friedman's house the next night and quizzed him about what he thought about schedules for learning like the one I'd been presented by the Lippold-Johnsons via Rabbi Offner. Her orders seemed as unyielding as the strictest Hasidic dictates—stricter, in fact.

"All along while we've been studying you've been letting me go at my own pace," I said, "not quizzing me unless I had questions, and spending more time teaching me by example at your dinner table than in your study."

He nodded. "More than everything," he said, "you wait. You choose the moment. You choose the setting. You wait for the child or student to be receptive, and then you deliver the message. The last thing you need to get across to the child or student is that you have to let her in on a great message, an important message, a true message.

"Beyond that, you need to tell your child or student that sharing is important, that arrogance is distasteful, that dishonesty is not acceptable, and lying is a no-no. You want to convince her that respecting elders is important as well as parents. You want to tell her that keeping a mitzvah, making a *bracha* [blessing], taking responsibility, that all of these things are true, correct, important, and necessary lessons and messages."

"That's an awful lot to expect a kid to take in," I said. "Especially if all I want to do is teach her her bat mitzvah," slurring the second to last word so it wasn't clear if I was saying "bar" or bat."

"You wait. You want her to have all these virtues, and you're impatient to tell her, to sit her down and say this is how you're supposed to be."

Hmm. It was sort of true. I was so excited by what I'd picked up over the previous year plus with Rabbi Friedman that I couldn't wait to begin cramming it down Mira's throat.

"You're impatient, and you want to sit them down and say, 'This is right, this is good, this is what I want from you.' But don't do that. Wait. You may have a good lesson, but the lesson has to become the child's property. It has to become what the child thinks, wants, believes. In order for all that to become the child's property, the child has to hear it when the child is ready to hear it, when the child is open to hearing, and when the child is most likely to absorb and ingest it, and make it part of their own thinking, feeling, and experience."

"How do you know when?" I asked. "I've always just operated on instinct."

He didn't disagree with me. "That's the romantic notion of the teacher being able to say the right thing at the right time; do the right thing at the right moment, in the right setting, and the right place."

"I never plan it out like that," I said. "I like the excitement that comes with winging it, like you said you do at some of your talks—see what the topic is when you get there and then just go."

"Fine. But we have to tell students what is correct, true, and right, show them that we've thought about what we're saying and have determined that this is the appropriate next lesson. And then we wait for them to create an opening. An opportunity when that message can be delivered to their best advantage."

I brought up again how grateful I was for him taking *me* on, especially considering my lifelong admitted penchant for getting rabbis riled up.

"I know what you mean," he said.

"You make rabbis mad?" I asked.

"Often." He smiled. "It seems to be one of my gifts. Especially among *Orthodox* rabbis."

"Do tell."

He paused. "Well, for example, many aren't real happy when I say it was good that Adam and Eve ate from the Tree of Knowledge."

"You're kidding. That's the original sin, for everybody!"

"But when God first created the world," he continued, "there was a certain Divine sameness to all things."

He opened his Hebrew Bible and read from Genesis, Chapter 1, verse 31, which translates into the King's English as "And God saw all that He had made, and behold, it was very good."

"In this world of sameness," Rabbi Friedman continued in his own words, "Adam and Eve were aware that they were naked but felt no shame."

I sat back, didn't say a word, just listened.

"After eating from the Tree of Knowledge—and it was a tree of knowledge, not of ignorance—Adam and Eve felt ashamed. What kind of knowledge could have caused this change in their perception of the world?

"The fruit of the Tree of Knowledge gave Adam and Eve the ability to make distinctions. Whereas before the world seemed one-dimensional, now it had many dimensions. In this new world of contrasts, all things were not the same. Some things were personal, others were not. Some things were private, some public. When they looked at themselves, they saw that they were naked—that is, they saw that without clothing, there was nothing to distinguish what was private about a human being from what was public. Their new awareness of the need for clothing caused Adam and Eve keen discomfort. That feeling of discomfort was shame.

"The sense of shame that originated with Adam and Eve was a healthy development. It gave them the ability to make distinctions—between private and public, modest and immodest, moral and immoral. Shame means that we recognize these borders. Shame is an essential part of God's plan, because it is the means to retaining innocence."

"But isn't shame terrible?" I asked. "If guilt is feeling terrible over something you've done, isn't shame feeling rotten over who you are? What does shame have to do with God's plan?"

"I mean shame in a positive sense," he said, "the kind of shame that brings humility, the kind of humility you feel when you're in the presence of someone superior to you. Because they ate from the Tree of Knowledge, Adam and Eve felt humility, and it was a healthy development. Before eating from the Tree of Knowledge, when the world still appeared to them as one-dimensional, they had not felt the contrast between the Creator and themselves. Now, for the first time, they realized the difference between 'small' and 'great.' "

"And that angers a lot of rabbis, hearing that?"

"Oh, you can't believe it. They argue, they yell, they stomp off."

"What do you do?"

He sat there silently, smiled, and opened his palms.

"But isn't that where the Torah says we lost our innocence, forget original sin, but that we had done sin number one and were kicked out of Eden for it?" I asked.

"Not at all," he said. "We could now choose to *become* innocent. Do you feel like a story?"

Of course I did.

"Okay. In the Russian village of Lubavitch, the eminent Rabbi Sholom Dov Ber was once gravely ill. His little boy, his only child, sat by the door to his father's room day and night. One day the doctor emerged from the rabbi's room with a sober expression that frightened the boy.

"The child ran to his teacher to ask what he could do. The teacher said, 'Tomorrow morning you will awaken very early and come with me to the cemetery. There I will tell you the prayers and psalms to recite at your grandfather's grave. We will both fast tomorrow, but you must tell no one.'

"The next morning the little boy arose while it was still dark, left his house, and joined his teacher. The snow was deep in Russia in the middle of winter. The child struggled to walk in the teacher's tracks.

"At the cemetery, he burst into tears and pleaded with his grandfather to intercede with the Almighty to save his father's life. As the dawn was breaking, the teacher tapped him on the shoulder and said, 'It's time to go back.'

"When they approached the town, they heard a shout. 'The fever has broken! The rabbi will recover!' The child looked at his teacher, who said, 'Thank God. But remember that this is a fast day for you. And no one must know.'

"Once again the child waited outside his father's room. When the doctor allowed him in for a few minutes, it was the first time in many days he had seen his father.

"His father spoke to the child. 'Have you had tea this morning?'

"The little boy was in a dilemma. He couldn't lie to his father. And he couldn't divulge that he was fasting. So he stood there silent. Fortunately, the doctor entered to tell him it was time to leave.

"This child's ability to remain silent demonstrated a profound degree of internal modesty. That he had fasted for his father's recovery remained private. When you achieve that degree of internal modesty you become receptive to your essence. What is that essence? Innocence."

And then Mrs. Friedman came into the study. "Are you staying for dinner, Nissan?" she asked me.

"Yes," I said.

"Well, come along, you two," she said to Rabbi Friedman and me, "while the chicken soup is still hot, and Moitel and Chaya and the kids are all here."

"Come," Rabbi Friedman said.

At dinner that night, for the first time since I was ten and following the lead of young Manis Friedman singing "Gedalia Goomberg," I was the first one banging out melodies on the table between courses, singing joyously.

I no longer exuded shame and sorrow for everything; the greatest gift Rabbi Friedman had given me was something I'd forgotten I'd ever had. Like the young Friedlicher Rebbe of long ago, I felt innocent.

"Help," I said to my friend Peggy over the phone. "HELP!"

"What's the matter?" she said from her home in Berkeley.

"Do you remember the haftarah trop? I'm tutoring this kid for her bat mitzvah, we're already behind, and I can't remember a single note!"

The tutor needed a tutor, fast, and my only hope was to drag Peggy into time traveling with me. Two decades before, Peggy had been a tenth-grade Saturday-school teacher under my aegis as a high school senior in overall charge of every twelve-year-old on his or her way to getting bar or bat mitzvahed that season.

Although Peggy was almost three years younger than me, we'd stayed close friends over the decades; her loyalty had never changed over the last several years as my life had slowly sunk into the mire.

"Don't panic," she said calmingly. "What's the *parsha*?"

"*Ki' Tetze.*"

"That was mine!" She began singing the haftarah from memory.

Thank you, God, thank you, God, thank you, God.

She would be visiting her folks in Minneapolis in a few weeks, she

said, and we could sit down then. I looked at the calendar. If I didn't
dink around, I could still learn this critical item on the bat mitzvah
agenda and not blow this little girl's big day. There were still several
months to the bat mitzvah, and if I learned how to read haftarah again,
passed the new notes along to Mira, and then applied them to that
text, we'd get there just in time. I hoped.

Two weeks later, Peggy sat across a table from me at French
Meadow restaurant. I took out my tape recorder while all around us
breakfast diners with tattoos and dreadlocks—Scandifarians, we called
them in Minnesota—ate their organic waffles.

Written by an unknown author during the Diaspora six centuries
before Jesus, Mira's and Peggy's shared haftarah portion preached of
unwavering faith in God to restore a homeland to Israel, no matter the
shit storm He'd already put the Jews through. God's love for His people, the Divine said as the portion concluded, may have bent at times
but would not break.

> For the mountains may move
> And the hills be shaken,
> But my loyalty shall never move from you,
> Nor my covenant of friendship be shaken
> Said the Lord, who takes you back in love.

"Nice," I said, pushing the tape recorder closer to Peggy. "Can you
sing it a couple more times?"

For the next several weeks I drilled myself on the haftarah until I was
reasonably sure I could get Mira through it.

Still, she was starting to become concerned. "Sherry Cohen's bat
mitzvah is only a week before mine, and she already knows all the
prayers *and* her haftarah," she said.

"Has she been memorizing everything instead of learning it?"

"Yeah. But who will know the difference?"

"I will. You will. The rabbi will. You'll never be able to read Torah or haftarah again if you just memorize it," I said as I stared nervously at the calendar laid before me on the dining room table. "Mira, you're going to kick everybody's ass."

"Really?"

"Promise. Now let's go over the words of the Torah reading again and then put all the notes under them. And then we'll talk about what the words actually mean. Did you read them all over in Hebrew and English?"

"They just seem like random laws," Mira said.

"Now we know the thing about men not being allowed to go into the army for a year if they've just been married," I said. "Read on, Gunga Din."

"Lo ya-cha-vole ray-chai-yeem va-ra-chev key-nefesh who cho-vale," she continued, reading the second sentence. " 'A handmill shall not be taken in pawn, for that would be taking someone's life in pawn.' What's a handmill?"

"It's what families used to use to make bread. You can't let them pawn it to you, because how else would they eat?"

"Hmm," she said, trying to make sense of pawning and handmills.

"There's an explanation in here," I said, trying to imitate Rabbi Friedman handing over a text. I passed her an old, classic jazz book called *Blues People* by the Jewish musician and historian Mezz Mezz-row. "Look up Charlie Parker and see if you find anything relating to this. He played saxophone just like you."

"I *know* Charlie Parker. We studied him in jazz class."

Putting the book away, she then went back to her Torah portion. *"Key ta-shey v'ray-ah-cha ma-a-sote mi-ooma low-ta-voe el-bay-to la-ah-vote ah-vo-toe. Ba-chootz ta-ah-mode v'ha-eesh asher ah-tah no-sheh bow yotzee aye-lecha et-ha-avot ha-chutza."* (When you make a loan of any sort to your neighbor, you must not enter his house to seize his pledge. You must remain outside, while the man to whom you made the loan brings the pledge out to you.) "Why?"

Remembering Rabbi Friedman coming up with his own interpretations of holy texts, I felt okay coming up with my own.

"You ever hear of a shame spiral, Mira?" I asked, remembering why I'd so liked this portion in the first place when I reread it with Rabbi Friedman. "You don't want to embarrass someone in front of his loved ones in his own house by making him pay you back a loan. It makes him feel bad, like a deadbeat, that he had to borrow from you in the first place."

And on and on we drilled, singing the Torah, haftarah, and prayers once a week, then come March twice a week, then in May three times a week, sometimes doing one of these sessions by phone.

"Is she going to be ready?" Lu asked me.

"She's a thoroughbred. She'll peak that Friday night. She's Seabiscuit, Man o' War, Seattle Slew, a Triple Crown winner. They'll hang a horseshoe of flowers around her neck when she's done."

"Okay," she said. "I'd rather they help me with the cooking."

The Lippold-Johnson dinners, meantime, felt as warm and joyous as ever. Why couldn't I, I wondered, deem this family and Rabbi Friedman's as the Jewish community I'd so longed for, the last thing I felt disconnected from? Why did I even *need* a whole synagogue, a modern shtetl to fit into? A Hasidic rabbi, his wife, and their fourteen kids in St. Paul; a Reform couple and their two kids in Minneapolis— wasn't that infinitely more community than I'd had amid Judaism since high school?

When the countdown hit T minus two weeks and counting, we moved over to the replica fake paper Torah I used to practice on when I was a kid, and Mira sped through her reading. A week later she went in to see Rabbi Offner, whom I still had studiously avoided, except for a wise-guy e-mail in which I jokingly told her I'd just realized I'd mistakenly taught Mira everything in Yiddish, not Hebrew. (The rabbi didn't respond.)

With the rabbi, she'd read directly from a real hand-inscribed Torah kept in Shir Tikvah's ark. She'd made some mistakes, she told me, but the rabbi had been very pleased with the couple of stutters—it meant, Rabbi Offner told Mira, she indeed knew how to read Torah and hadn't simply flawlessly memorized the thing like a top-forty tune. Already, the rabbi had told her, she had something in mind for her to chant on Yom Kippur.

"Told ya," I said, and Mira beamed, though not half as brightly as I did.

"While I'm reading on Saturday morning I want you to have an aliyah," she said, meaning I'd be one of the five people—usually relatives—called to the Torah individually to say the blessings before and after each of the sections the *parsha* had been divided into. I hadn't had an aliyah since the Hasidim at Rabbi Friedman's shul had pushed me forward for my first epiphany. Yet after Mira asked me, I knew it was truly possible to wear an ear-to-ear grin.

"I'd be honored," I said.

21

THE BAT MITZVAH, CHARLIE PARKER, AND AMEN

Friday night services, the prelude to tomorrow morning's major action of Mira's bat mitzvah, went flawlessly. Rabbi Offner didn't seem so intimidating after all—her first act was presenting Mira with a blue tallis, and some not mawkish words about its meaning.

Rabbi Offner offered a sermon that, after a few seconds, I realized hit on many topics that Rabbi Friedman had discussed with me over the previous year and a half. I was struck with the notion that here were two oddly kindred, wise spirits and twinges of shame over my own hubris in writing her off so reflexively.

That night I could barely sleep. What if Mira forgot everything Saturday morning? What if I forgot how to sing my aliyah before one of her Torah readings? Why had I invited my parents?

When I got to the shul that Saturday morning, it was filled with a potpourri of Shir Tikvah Jews, some in jeans, their heads and shoulders uncovered. Others were in formal suits wearing yarmulkes and tallises, and a third contingent sported every sartorial and religious combination between.

Mira's extended family sat in the front rows, while a collection of Lu's and Bruce's friends filled the sanctuary, which held perhaps two hundred. I'd come with half a dozen of my pals who also knew Bruce and Lu and who'd never seen a bar or bat mitzvah but who had *Yiddishe hartzes.*

Finally, right before services started, I saw my parents slip in through a side door and take seats in the back row. My father, out of respect for what he thought would be the old-style Reform service, hadn't brought his yarmulke or tallis. Ironically, half the congregation, including the women, were wearing theirs.

I started shaking—not out of nervousness but excitement. The epiphany was as bright as the holy light over the ark. *They came.*

Looking over my shoulder, I was amazed at how gentle my father looked. I'd always seen and admired him above all else for his toughness, his *Jewish* toughness. My father had taught me the importance of being willing to fight with pride for one's Jewishness, and I had watched with awe as he, in his seventies, would still put on boxing gloves and pound out a staccato rhythm on the very-difficult-to-master speed bag at the Jewish Community Center health club. It was the feat of a lifetime of practiced coordination I'd never been able to accomplish, even after months of boxing training with a professional.

Well, *he* was still here, for me, in the back row. I couldn't have felt prouder.

I turned around and watched Mira take the bimah and float flawlessly through the Shabbat morning prayers. After she gave a smart, funny, and wise interpretation of her Torah portion, a sermon she'd refused to show me, I glowed as if I was her own father. And I was alight with *nachas* and projected *yichus* when it became clear she'd unearthed the colorful explanation of a piece of Yiddishkeit in her Torah portion by using the text I'd nonchalantly given to her with little explanation during her studies.

Just as Rabbi Friedman made me find my own answers in the books he lent me without explanation, the girl who seemed as tall as her own tenor saxophone explained a particular mitzvah with Mezz Mezzrow's *Blues People*. She said:

> There is a law in my Torah portion that you cannot take a person's means of living in pawn. It gives the example of a bread maker, but it applies to everyone. Even the famous saxophone player Charlie Parker.
>
> Charlie Parker was once far in debt and he pawned his saxophone. Luckily, he had a plastic sax, so he didn't have to forfeit any concerts. He even played one of his best concerts on his plastic sax. Eventually one of his fans got the saxophone back to him, and the plastic one is now in the Jazz Hall of Fame.
>
> If this law from the Torah was one of our laws now, this would never have been a problem. No pawnbroker would have been allowed to take Charlie Parker's saxophone.

Mira had conquered Yiddishkeit as well as my old secular definition of a warm and humane mensch.

Yet now the toughest task was at hand. When the Torah came out of the ark and was unfurled, she cruised through the first few portions with at most one or two barely noticeable hesitations—proof to the congregation she hadn't memorized her portion but knew how to read the thing and was deducing difficult combinations of letters.

When I was called to the Torah to say my blessings before and after she read—"*Ya-a-mod, Nissan ben Mordechai ben vu Chaya*" (Come forward, Nissan, son of Markle and Charlotte)—I bounded up the stairs of the bimah. Radiating pride and avuncular love, I spontaneously gave my charge the "peace out" symbol that slugger Sammy Sosa of the Chicago Cubs famously gives every time he hits another home run. I hadn't beamed like this since my aliyah at Rabbi Friedman's Hasidic shul.

Everyone in the congregation saw it and I heard joy in their chortles. Mira laughed at me from atop the wooden box behind the podium, invisible to the congregation, that raised her head above the Torah and into full view of her audience.

Mira pointed with the silver *yod* to her place in the Torah, and I wrapped my finger around the end of my tallis and kissed the spot with it. My surprise gift to my father, I'd decided the night before, was to sing my aliyah the old Ashkenazic shtetl way, sung only by the Jews who perished in the Holocaust, the Hasidim and stubborn old-timers like himself.

Once again, I pronounced the letter that was now known universally known as *taf* and pronounced with a hard *t*.

My voice boomed out over the congregation in a way I couldn't remember happening in decades as I chanted, *"Barchu Es Adonai Hamvorach!"*

I continued on, looking out and directly catching my father's eye. I then bowed slightly toward him, flashing the prayer book page that bore the blessing over the Torah that I was chanting by heart. It was clear to all in the sanctuary to whom I was paying homage, though most in the young congregation couldn't figure out why I was seemingly mispronouncing some familiar words in the oft-repeated prayer. *"V'Na-San Lanoo es Torah-so. Baruch atah adonai—no-sane ha-Torah."*

In the back row, my father unfurled his arms and smiled broadly. The journey had all been worthwhile. Mira cruised through her next several lines, and then it was my turn to touch the Torah again with my tallis and continue the prayer every aliyah chanted following each reading. *"Asher nassan lanu Torah emes, v'ha-yay olam, nata b'so-chanu. Baruch atah adonai, no-sane ha-Torah."*

The congregation intoned, *"Ah-maaay-en,"* and I could pick out my father's deep bass.

When I was finished, I joined my parents in the back row, and my father put his arm behind my shoulder and atop my chair. We sat there wordlessly until the end, when Mira gave her thank yous: "Thank you, Neal Karlen, for being my tutor and making preparing for my bat mitzvah as much of an experience as actually having it."

"Good going, boychick," my father said proudly.

I thought about how we had been oddly brought together again by an old Hasidic rabbi with a Sam Spade fedora.

"As they say in the Talmud, Dad," I responded, *"Ayn somchin al haness."* (You can't wait for a miracle.)

"Amen," he said.

"Amen," I repeated after him.

ABOUT THE AUTHOR

NEAL KARLEN writes regularly for *The New York Times* and has been a staff writer for *Newsweek* and *Rolling Stone*. He has also written for *The New Yorker, Esquire, GQ,* the *Forward* and *Olam*. He has written five books on popular culture, and collaborated on Henny Youngman's autobiography and on a rock opera with the musician Prince. A lecturer at the University of Minnesota Journalism School, he lives in his native Minnesota.